The Innovative Pharmacy

The Innovative Pharmacy

How to Build an 8-Figure Pharmacy
One Idea at a Time

Jonathan Adly, PharmD
Meghan Lui, PharmD

ISBN: 979-8-9945496-0-5 (paperback)

Published by TJM Labs
Printed in the United States of America

First edition

Acknowledgements

To the customers of TJM Labs, many of whom we consider friends. Thank you for believing in us. You constantly inspire us.
This book wouldn't be possible without you. Your innovation and creativity are a model for the industry. We see this book as a mirror, reflecting and spreading your great work.

Thank you.

Table of Contents

Introduction

> "There are those who seek knowledge for the sake of knowledge; that is Curiosity.
>
> There are those who seek knowledge to be known by others; that is Vanity.
>
> There are those who seek knowledge in order to serve; that is Love."
>
> — Bernard of Clairvaux

We wrote this book for a simple reason: to help pharmacies succeed.

The pharmacy business is tough right now. One of the largest pharmacy chains in the U.S. recently declared bankruptcy. Another was taken private, with plans to break it up and sell the pieces. PBMs routinely reimburse pharmacies below cost. Labor expenses continue to rise. And between large insurers and health systems, patients often have little choice in where they can go.

It can feel impossible to get ahead. But it's not.

We know how to win in this environment, and this book will show you how. We know because we've worked with hundreds of pharmacies across the U.S.

and Canada. We've been embedded in their operations and have seen firsthand what separates struggling pharmacies from truly exceptional ones.

This isn't a typical business book that pushes one specific method that worked for one company. This book is different. We're going to show you the many different ways pharmacies succeed. The only common thread is innovation. Beyond that, their paths are all unique.

We aren't going to give you a rigid, step-by-step plan. We won't recommend specific vendors or prescribe a single "best" process. In a dynamic business like pharmacy, what works today may not work six months from now. Instead, we'll give you frameworks and principles that endure.

Our company, TJM Labs, builds AI agents that automate pharmacy workflows. These systems handle administrative work like processing faxes and e-prescriptions, managing refills, and performing benefits investigations. This gives us a unique window into what actually makes a pharmacy successful.

Often, a pharmacy comes to us right after a period of rapid growth. They can no longer keep up with hiring and need automation to handle the volume. We've seen partners 10× their business in a single year.

Our vantage point is unique. Unlike typical tech vendors with limited contact with their clients, we operate with a dual-expert™ model. A pharmacist and an engineer from our team work directly with each pharmacy to understand their operations and build the right automation. We don't just see the outside of a successful business—we see the core of what makes it work. It's a deep partnership, where their success is our success.

Our perspective goes beyond our company. We are both pharmacists who have spent decades in the industry. Jonathan Adly has deep experience in 340B and served as an executive at a large digital pharmacy. Meghan Lui brings extensive operational expertise from working within the complex Canadian pharmacy landscape. Together, our backgrounds span pharmacy, engineering, operations, and business.

As we share what has made our partners successful, we will change certain details to protect their trade secrets. The goal isn't for you to copy their exact playbook—it wouldn't work for your business anyway. The goal is to give you the principles behind their success so you can build your own.

This book is made up of ten chapters. Each chapter introduces a key principle, explains an operational framework, and shows what excellent execution looks like in practice.

We have a saying on our team: you only learn by doing.

That goes for you, too. This book contains a lot of knowledge, but knowledge alone isn't enough. To get results, you need to take action.

We want to help you succeed. Let's do this together.

If you have a friend who's also a pharmacy leader, ask them to be your accountability partner. If not, I will be.

Take a moment right now and send me a message.

It's your first step.

Email: Jonathan@tjmlabs.com

Subject: I am reading The Innovative Pharmacy

Body:

> "Hi Jonathan,
>
> I just started your book and I'm ready to get to work. I'd like your help keeping me on track. Looking forward to taking action together.
>
> [Your name]"

Or text me: 347-861-1051

To make this book as practical as possible, each chapter begins with a short three-bullet summary. This isn't a novel. We want you to know the key ideas upfront so you can apply them to your business as you read. At the end of each chapter, a Now What? section gives you immediate, actionable steps.

We promise that no matter what kind of pharmacy you run—community, long-term care, specialty, digital, or compounding—this book will be relevant. We've intentionally included examples from every segment of the industry. These frameworks are for you.

1

The Special Customer

- Success is about serving the right customers.
- Your Ideal Customer Profile is often not who you think it is.
- Shrinking your customer base to focus on a highly profitable niche can unlock explosive growth and long-term resilience.

The Allure of "More"

Many of us started our careers in chain pharmacies. I got my start as an intern at a busy Rite Aid, where the definition of success was simple: more. More scripts, more vaccines, more patients on auto-refill. The mantra was volume, volume, volume. Any person who walked through the door was a customer, and every script was a good script.

So when pharmacists open their own store, they often copy this model. The logic seems sound: Everyone knows the big chains offer terrible service. If I just provide a better experience, I'll win. But that logic is a trap.

Being busy is not the same as being profitable. Every prescription has a real cost attached—not just the drug, but the labor, the time, and the overhead required to fill it. Think about it. Would you rather own a pharmacy that fills a million scripts a day and loses one dollar on each, or one that fills 100 scripts a day and makes $1,000 on each? The answer is obvious.

This brings us to the single most important lesson: you must know your "special customer."

Failing to define this customer is a trap we see pharmacies fall into over and over. In the business world, this concept has a fancy acronym: ICP, or Ideal Customer Profile. Don't let the MBA-talk fool you. It simply means knowing your special customer.

Identifying and focusing on this customer is the first real step toward building an 8-figure pharmacy.

Let me tell you a story about a pharmacy that fell into this trap. They had everything you could want on the surface—venture capital, a slick mobile app, and thousands of users. But they were losing millions.

Then, they found their special customer. In less than two years, they skyrocketed to over $100 million in revenue with healthy profit margins.

The Slick App Fallacy

We'll call our case study "FastRx." We changed their name because their current niche is highly competitive. Their model was built for the modern consumer—an easy-to-use mobile app for ordering refills, free same-day delivery in a major city, and friendly branding. Their target customer was anyone and everyone with a prescription.

The founder was a former supervising pharmacist at a major chain. He saw how much patients hated the experience and knew it was a real problem. Almost every single customer he interacted with didn't like their pharmacy.

So, he recruited a brilliant engineer to—in their words— "fix pharmacy." They managed to raise a healthy amount of venture capital for their new, modern pharmacy. They executed their plan perfectly.

Beautiful branding, good marketing, the perfect mobile app with an amazing user experience. On paper, they were crushing it. Patient numbers grew 50% month-over-month. The app had tens of thousands of downloads. They were the poster child for the innovative pharmacy.

But the numbers told a very different story.

They had extremely low margins. Most of their customers were on low-margin generics. PBM reimbursements were brutal.

They also had incredibly high costs. Free delivery was expensive. Marketing costs to acquire each new patient were high. The operational costs to manage thousands of small orders were crushing them.

For every $1 of revenue they brought in, they were spending $2.50.

They looked like a successful tech company from the outside but were really a failing pharmacy. The more they grew, the faster they lost money.

Finding Your Special Customer

The team at FastRx lived the story of many pharmacies—only they lived it in fast-forward. But to their credit, while other, similar companies were failing, they refused to give up. FastRx faced the hard truth: their business model was broken. They had to stop asking:

How can we get more customers?

and start asking a much better question:

Who should our customers be?

They shifted their focus away from fancy marketing and toward finding someone with a painful problem they could solve profitably. This is the core task for any innovative pharmacy.

So, how do you find your special customer? It's a discovery process that starts in one of two places: looking inward at what you already have, or looking outward for new opportunities.

Step 1: Look at Your Books

For an established pharmacy, the answer might already be in your data. Do you have a "special customer" hiding in plain sight? It could be a local long-term care facility, a telehealth clinic specializing in longevity, or even a summer camp that sends you all its attendee prescriptions.

Run a report of your most profitable accounts—not by revenue, but by margin. What do they look like? If you find a group that is highly profitable and easy to serve, you've struck gold.

That's your ICP. The search is over. Now you can focus all your energy on finding more customers exactly like them.

Step 2: Start a Discovery Mission

Most pharmacies, however, don't find a hidden gem in their books. That's when you need to look outward. This is exactly what the FastRx team did.

Their leadership team went to industry conferences—not to sell their services, but to listen. Their goal was to talk to anyone and everyone to discover who might need a pharmacy partner in a way they hadn't considered.

During one lunch, they met an executive from a tiny pharmaceutical manufacturer. He complained about how impossible it was to get their new, high-cost, high-touch drug to patients and keep them on it.

The big retail pharmacies didn't care about the patient experience, and PBMs added endless friction. The manufacturer was losing millions simply because they couldn't find a pharmacy that cared.

That was it. That was their "special customer."

They pitched a solution: they would become the manufacturer's dream pharmacy. They offered a "white-glove" service that handled everything—benefits investigation, patient onboarding, adherence coaching, and data reporting. They became an extension of the manufacturer's team.

The economics were completely transformed. The manufacturer gave them the drug at a steep discount and paid a significant service fee for each patient.

Their margin went from losing a few dollars on each

script to gaining hundreds of dollars per script.

More importantly, they made a critical decision: they shut down their consumer-facing app and stopped all general marketing. To win, they had to go all-in on serving this special customer.

Once the model was proven, they found a second manufacturer, then a third, and a fourth.

Their ICP became clear: small pharmaceutical manufacturers (under $1 billion market cap) with complex, high-touch drugs.

Their understanding of this customer became so sophisticated that they started targeting companies before their drug even got FDA approval.

They even learned that the best point of contact was the Chief Financial Officer—the person who feels the pain of lost revenue the most.

As you'd expect, their patient count dropped by over 90%. But their profitability exploded.

They became an 8-figure business in 18 months by focusing entirely on their special customer.

•••

The Framework: Finding Your Special Customer

The story of FastRx isn't just about rare drugs. It's about a way of thinking that transformed their business—and it can transform yours, too. It comes down to clearly defining two things: your Ideal Customer Profile (ICP) and your Total Addressable Market (TAM). Your ICP isn't just a demographic. It's the specific person or organization that gets the most value from what you uniquely offer and, in return, provides the most value back to your business.

Here is a simple framework to find yours.

Part 1: Define Your Ideal Customer Profile (ICP)

Your ICP sits at the intersection of three simple questions:

Who is my most profitable customer?

Forget revenue. Look at net profit. Pull the data and analyze who is actually making you money. Is it the high-volume, low-margin generic prescriptions, or the smaller group of patients on more complex medications? The numbers don't lie. Start here.

What problem do I uniquely solve?

What are you better at than any other pharmacy in town? Be honest. Your unique ability is the foundation of your value.

- **Speed**: Prescriptions ready in 10 minutes or less.
- **Expertise**: The local authority on hormone replacement therapy.
- **Convenience**: The only pharmacy that delivers to the rural side of the county.
- **Administrative Relief**: We remove the burden of prior authorizations for Dr. Smith's office.

Who values that solution the most?

This is where it all comes together. Who is willing to pay for your unique solution to their problem?

For FastRx, their slick app was a "nice-to-have" for busy consumers. But for the drug manufacturer, their "white-glove" service solved a multi-million-dollar problem. The manufacturer valued that solution far more than any individual patient ever could.

Your special customer is the one who sees your unique strength as a must-have, not a nice-to-have.

Part 2: Define Your Total Addressable Market (TAM)

Once you know who you're looking for, you need to know how many of them there are. This is your TAM. Most pharmacies get this wrong. The common mistake is to define your TAM too broadly, like "everyone within a 10-mile radius." This is a useless metric. You can't effectively market to everyone. A better approach is to be narrow and deep. Your TAM is the total number of your ideal customers within your reach.

- **Bad TAM**: All seniors in our city.
- **Good TAM**: The 350 residents of the Golden Years assisted living facility two blocks away.
- **Bad TAM**: All busy professionals.
- **Good TAM**: The 500 employees at the self-insured law firm downtown who value premium service and convenience.

A small pond where you are the big fish is infinitely better than an ocean where you are just another drop of water.

A clearly defined TAM gives you a target. It turns a vague goal ("grow the business") into a specific mission: win the business of all three dermatology clinics in our medical district.

•••

Now What?

A framework is only useful if you use it. Theory is great, but action is what builds an 8-figure business. Here are three simple, powerful actions you can take this week.

Your One-Hour Assignment: The Profit Report

This is non-negotiable. Block out one hour this week and run a report of your top 50 customers. But here's the crucial step: sort it by net profit, not revenue. Who is actually making you money? Look for patterns. Is it a specific doctor's office? A group of patients on a particular drug? A company whose employees all use your pharmacy? The clues to your most valuable customer are already in your computer. Your job is to go find them.

Make Space for Growth: Fire a Customer Segment

You can't serve your special customer if your team's time is drained by the wrong ones. Identify the single biggest time-suck in your pharmacy that produces the least profit. It could be the price-shoppers who require five phone calls for a $2 margin. Make a conscious decision to "fire" this segment. This doesn't mean being rude; it means you stop investing your marketing, your time, and your energy into keeping them. You need to clear the decks to make room for the customers who will actually grow your business.

Go on a Problem Hunt

Schedule a 30-minute brainstorming session with your team.

Prompt: What is a painful problem we could solve for another business?

Think about local employers, specialist medical clinics, veterinarians, or senior living facilities. What is a constant, expensive headache they face related to medication or patient care? And how could you offer a service that makes that headache disappear?

Don't think about products; think about solving problems. The biggest problem you find could be your next special customer.

•••

Now that you've identified your special customer, the next step is to build a sales and marketing machine to find more of them. We'll show you how in the next chapter.

2

Why Being Known Isn't Enough

- Marketing makes you visible. Sales makes you money.
- Know your ICP's pain so well that choosing you becomes inevitable.
- Marketing amplifies what sales proves.

The Pharmacy No One Had Heard Of

In 2024, a pharmacy you'd never heard of was quietly growing faster than almost anyone in the industry. Giftwell wasn't on Instagram. They weren't running Facebook ads. They weren't sponsoring the big pharmacy conferences. No slick brand campaign. No viral content. No "awareness strategy."

If you asked a random pharmacist at ASHP or a patient on the street, "Have you heard of Giftwell?" the answer would be a blank stare.

And yet, they grew 10x in a single year.

They understood something most pharmacies get backwards.

Marketing makes you known. Sales makes you rich.

While other startups were burning cash on brand consultants and social media managers, Giftwell was doing something radically different. They built a large sales organization and went directly to their customers, one conversation at a time.

They didn't wait to be discovered. They didn't hope their ads would work. They showed up where their ideal customers were, understood their pain deeply, and solved it.

By the time the industry started hearing about Giftwell in newsletters and on podcasts, they were already an 8-figure business.

Marketing didn't get them there. Sales did.

Let me tell you their story.

The Colonoscopy Crisis

The founding team at Giftwell didn't start with a product looking for a market. They started with a market screaming for a solution.

They identified their ICP with surgical precision: gastroenterology offices performing colonoscopies.

Here's why this was brilliant.

A colonoscopy is a revenue-generating procedure. It brings in anywhere from $1,500 to $3,000 per procedure for the practice. But there's a fragile dependency: the patient must complete a bowel prep the night before. No prep, no procedure.

And here's where the nightmare begins for GI offices.

- The patient gets the prescription for the bowel prep.
- They take it to their local pharmacy.
- The pharmacy is out of stock, insurance denies it, or the patient sees the $80 co-pay.
- The medication isn't picked up or arrives too late.

The patient shows up unprepared. The procedure gets canceled.

The practice loses $1,500 to $3,000 in revenue. The scheduler has to find another slot. The physician's time is wasted. The patient is frustrated and embarrassed.

And the cycle often repeats when they reschedule.

For a busy GI practice doing 20 colonoscopies a day, even a 10% cancellation rate due to medication issues is $30,000 to $60,000 in lost monthly revenue.

That's real money. That's a crisis.

Giftwell's founding team saw this problem and asked the most important question in business: Who is in the most pain, and how do we make that pain disappear?

The answer was clear. GI offices were hemorrhaging revenue because patients couldn't reliably get a simple bowel prep medication. Giftwell's value proposition was elegantly simple:

> "We make sure your patients get their bowel prep on time, every time. No more canceled procedures."

They didn't need to convince GI administrators that this was a problem. The problem was already keeping them up at night. Giftwell just had to prove they could solve it.

The Sales Machine, Not the Marketing Engine

Most pharmacy startups follow a predictable path. They build a product, create a brand, launch a website, start running ads, post on social media, and hope customers show up.

Giftwell took the opposite approach. They built a large sales organization from day one. Not marketers. Salespeople.

Their playbook was simple and brutally effective.

Step 1: Build the target list

They identified every gastroenterology office within their serviceable area. Not hospitals. Not general practitioners. GI offices. That was the list.

Step 2: Direct outreach

Their sales team made calls, sent emails, and showed up in person to talk to practice administrators and physicians. Not mass emails. Not automated campaigns. Personal, direct contact.

Step 3: Lead with the pain

The opening line of every conversation was some version of:

> "How many procedures did you cancel last month because patients couldn't get their bowel prep?"

The answer was always painful. And once the administrator admitted the problem, the sale was already halfway done.

Step 4: Prove it with a pilot

Giftwell didn't ask for a long-term contract upfront.

They said, "Let us handle bowel prep for your next 10 patients. We'll show you the results in 30 days. If it works, we'll talk about a bigger partnership."

Pilots removed risk. And the results spoke for themselves.

Patients got their medications on time. Procedures didn't get canceled. The GI office made more money.

Step 5: Close the contract

Once the pilot worked, the decision was easy. Giftwell became the exclusive bowel prep provider for the practice.

Here's what's important:

Giftwell didn't need to be famous. They didn't need thousands of social media followers or glowing press coverage. They needed to be indispensable to GI offices. And they were.

No one outside of gastroenterology had heard of them. And that was the point. They weren't trying to be known by everyone. They were trying to be the obvious choice for their ICP.

Do It Again: The Formula Proven

Once the GI office model was humming and generating serious revenue, Giftwell did something smart. They asked, "Who else has this exact same pain?"

The answer: pharmaceutical companies running direct-to-patient programs.

Here's the pattern they saw:

Pharma companies spend hundreds of millions of dollars getting a drug through FDA approval. But approval is only half the battle. The drug has to actually reach patients. And for specialty medications, high-cost drugs, or drugs requiring complex prior authorizations, the traditional retail pharmacy model is a disaster.

Patients get frustrated. They abandon therapy. The pharma company loses revenue. The clinical outcomes the drug was designed to achieve never happen.

It's the same problem Giftwell solved for GI offices, just in a different form. A painful, expensive gap between the prescription being written and the patient actually getting the medication.

Giftwell reused the exact same playbook.

They built a target list of pharmaceutical companies with specialty drugs. Their sales team reached out directly to decision-makers: VPs of Patient Services, Heads of Market Access, Chief Financial Officers.

The pitch was tailored but the structure was identical: "Your patients are abandoning therapy because they can't navigate the complexity. We solve that. Let us run a pilot."

They offered white-glove service: benefits investigation, prior authorization management, patient onboarding, adherence coaching, and data reporting. They made the pharma company's drug access problem disappear.

And again, they closed deal after deal. Not through marketing. Through direct sales and flawless execution.

The 10x Result

In one year, Giftwell grew 10x.

How? A large, disciplined sales organization laser-focused on two highly specific ICPs: GI offices and pharmaceutical companies.

They had a tiny marketing footprint. Almost zero brand awareness outside their niches.

If you weren't a GI administrator or a pharma market access director, you'd never heard of them.

And that was perfectly fine.

Because those two groups? They knew exactly who Giftwell was. And they were writing big checks.

Only after Giftwell crossed into 8-figures did they start appearing in industry newsletters, and podcasts. By then, they had hundreds of customers, billions in revenue, and a proven, repeatable growth engine.

> Marketing didn't create that growth. Marketing made the growth more efficient.

When you're already closing 50 deals a year through direct sales, marketing helps deal #51 comes easier because the prospect has now heard your name before the first call. But marketing doesn't replace the work of sales. It amplifies it.

Giftwell proved something that most pharmacy owners don't want to hear: You don't have an awareness problem. You have a sales problem.

•••

The Framework: The Sales-First Growth System

The story of Giftwell isn't about luck or a hot market. It's about a disciplined approach to growth that any pharmacy can replicate. You don't need venture capital. You don't need a huge team. You just need to stop spending money on awareness and start investing in direct sales.

Part 1: Start With Sales, Not Awareness

Most pharmacies think growth happens like this:

- Build a brand
- Run ads and post on social media
- Generate awareness
- Hope customers come to you

Giftwell proved it actually works like this:

1. Identify your ICP (you did this in Chapter 1)
2. Understand their painful, expensive problem
3. Go directly to them and solve it
4. Repeat until you have proof
5. Add marketing to make sales easier at scale (Optional)

The key insight: Your ICP already exists. They're already in pain. You don't need to make them aware of you. You need to show up where they are and prove you can solve their problem.

Think about Giftwell and GI offices. Did GI administrators need to be convinced that canceled colonoscopies were a problem? No. They lived that problem every single day. Giftwell just had to prove they could fix it.

That's the power of selling to a well-defined ICP. The problem is already real. The pain is already expensive. You're not creating demand. You're capturing it.

Part 2: Build Your ICP Pain Map

Before you spend a single dollar on ads or brand awareness, you need to answer four questions about your ICP. These questions will form the foundation of your entire sales strategy.

Question 1: What is their expensive problem?

Not "they need prescriptions filled." That's too generic. Every patient needs prescriptions filled. That's not a painful problem; that's just a transaction.

Find the problem that costs your ICP real money or creates real pain when it goes unsolved.

For GI offices, it was canceled procedures costing thousands of dollars per day. For pharma companies, it was patient abandonment costing millions in lost revenue and failed market access strategies.

For your ICP, what is it?

Here's how to find out. Call three of your current

best customers.

Ask them: “What problem were you trying to solve when you started working with us? What was that problem costing you before we fixed it?”

Listen carefully. Write down their exact words. That’s your sales pitch.

Question 2: Where do they congregate?

Your ICP isn’t scattered randomly across the country. They gather in specific places, both physical and digital.

- What professional associations do they join?
- What conferences do they attend?
- What LinkedIn groups are they active in?
- What industry publications do they read?
- Who do they already trust and listen to?

Giftwell didn’t need to figure out how to reach GI administrators through generic Facebook ads. They just showed up at the American Society for Gastrointestinal Endoscopy (ASGE) conferences and joined the online communities where GI practice managers shared best practices.

Your ICP is already congregating somewhere. Find those places.

Question 3: Who is the decision-maker?

This is where most pharmacies get it wrong. They assume the decision-maker is the most obvious person, the physician, the patient, the C-suite executive, but that's often not true.

For GI offices, the physician writes the prescription, but the practice administrator decides which pharmacy to partner with for bowel prep fulfillment. The administrator feels the pain of lost revenue and wasted scheduling time.

For pharma companies, it's not always the Chief Medical Officer. Often, it's the VP of Patient Services or the CFO, because they're the ones measured on patient adherence and revenue per drug.

Find the person who feels the pain of the problem most acutely and who has the authority to write a check to make it go away. That's your decision-maker.

Question 4: What is their buying process?

- How does your ICP actually make purchasing decisions?
- Do they need to see a pilot first, or can they commit immediately?
- What metrics do they care about? Cost savings? Time savings? Patient outcomes? Completion rates?
- How long is the sales cycle? One month? Six

months?
- Do they need internal approvals, or can one person say yes?

Understanding the buying process lets you design a sales approach that matches their decision-making reality.

Giftwell knew that GI offices would never commit to an exclusive partnership without proof, so they always led with a low-risk pilot. That insight dramatically shortened their sales cycle.

Part 3: The Five-Step Sales Playbook

Once you've mapped your ICP's pain, you're ready to execute. Here's an example playbook that you can use.

Step 1: Build your target list (25-100 ICPs to start)

Open a spreadsheet or a simple CRM. Create these columns:

- Company/Organization Name
- Decision-Maker Name and Title
- Contact Information (email, phone, LinkedIn)
- Specific Pain Points (from your research)

- Status (Not Contacted, Reached Out, Meeting Scheduled, Pilot Running, Closed)

Start with 25 targets. Do the research. Use LinkedIn, association directories, Google, referrals from current customers. Find the decision-maker's name and direct contact information.

This target list is your sales pipeline. Everything starts here.

Step 2: Craft your direct pitch

You need one sentence that makes your ICP lean forward. Here's the formula:

> "We help [ICP] avoid [expensive problem] by [solution], which results in [measurable outcome]."

Giftwell's pitch to GI offices: "We help gastroenterology practices avoid canceled colonoscopies by ensuring patients receive bowel prep medications on time, which eliminates revenue loss from procedure cancellations."

Notice what this does. It names the ICP. It highlights their painful problem. It describes the solution. And it ties directly to a measurable business outcome they care about.

Make your pitch specific, measurable, and tied to their pain. Not "we're a great pharmacy." Not "we offer excellent service." Those are meaningless. Lead with their pain and your solution.

Step 3: Make direct contact

This is where most pharmacy owners fail. They post on social media. They tweak their website. They run Google Ads. And they wonder why nothing happens.

Stop. Direct outreach is how deals get done.

Pick up the phone. Send a personalized email. Message them on LinkedIn. Ask a mutual connection for a warm introduction. Show up at the conference they're attending.

Your goal is simple: book a 15-minute discovery call. Here's a proven email script:

> Subject: About [their specific challenge]
>
> "Hi [Name],
>
> I work with [ICP type] who often struggle with [expensive problem]. I noticed [specific observation about their organization] and thought there might be an opportunity to help.
>
> Would you be open to a 15-minute call this week to discuss how you're currently handling [problem]? I'd love to learn more about your situation.
>
> Best,
>
> [Your Name]"

Short. Direct. Respectful of their time. Focused on their problem, not your product.

Track every contact. Note what works. Refine your approach. Most sales happen between the 5th and 12th touchpoint, so don't give up after one email.

Step 4: The discovery call and pilot offer

You got the meeting. Great. Now resist the urge to pitch immediately.

Spend the first 10 minutes listening. Ask open-ended questions:

- "What's your biggest challenge with [area related to your solution]?"
- "How are you currently handling [the problem]?"
- "What does it cost you when [problem] goes wrong?"
- "Have you tried other solutions? What didn't work?"

Let them talk. Take notes. Understand their specific pain in their own words.

Only after you've listened should you explain how you solve their problem. And even then, don't ask for a big commitment.

End with a pilot offer:

> "Here's what I'd suggest. Let's start with [small, defined scope]. We'll run this for 30 days and

show you the results. If it works as well as I think it will, we can talk about a longer-term partnership. If it doesn't, no hard feelings. Does that sound reasonable?"

Pilots remove risk. They let you prove your value before asking for a major commitment. We used this approach religiously in TJM labs, and it worked every time.

Step 5: Systematize and scale

Once you've closed 5-10 customers using this exact process, you have something incredibly valuable: a repeatable sales motion.

Now you can scale.

Document everything. Write down your pitch. Create email templates. Build a script for discovery calls. Design a standard pilot agreement.

Hire or train someone to replicate what you just did. Instead of you making 5 calls a week, your sales team makes 50.

This is how Giftwell went from a few customers to hundreds. They didn't rely on the founder's charisma or luck. They built a system that anyone on their team could execute.

Part 4: When Marketing Finally Makes Sense

Let me be clear: I'm not saying marketing is useless. I'm saying it's useless until you've built a proven sales engine.

Marketing becomes valuable after you've done the hard work of direct sales. Here's when you know you're ready to invest in marketing:

- You've closed 20+ ICP customers through direct sales
- You have clear proof points, case studies, and testimonials
- Your sales team is consistently saying, "Prospects have never heard of us, so every call starts from zero trust"
- You're ready to scale beyond your personal network and referrals

At that point, marketing isn't about creating demand. It's about making your sales process more efficient.

When a prospect has already heard of you, read an article you wrote, or seen you speak at a conference, the first sales call is easier. They come in with some baseline trust.

Here's the right kind of marketing for B2B pharmacy sales:

- **Thought leadership**: Write articles, publish white papers, speak at industry conferences, appear on podcasts. This is exactly what Giftwell did once they hit 8-figures. By then, they had the credibility to speak with authority about GI pharmacy partnerships and specialty drug access.
- **Case studies**: "How We Helped [GI Office Name] Eliminate 95% of Procedure Cancellations." Real stories with real numbers. These become powerful sales tools.
- **Strategic partnerships**: Co-market with professional associations, industry groups, or complementary vendors. If you serve GI offices, partner with the gastroenterology association to co-host a webinar on reducing procedure cancellations.
- **Targeted content**: A monthly newsletter for GI practice administrators with operational tips and industry insights. Not a generic newsletter for "healthcare professionals." Targeted. Specific.
- **Referral programs**: Your best marketing is your current customers telling their peers about you. Incentivize referrals. Make it easy for happy customers to introduce you.

Here's what NOT to spend money on before you have a proven sales engine:

- Broad social media ad campaigns
- Generic "brand awareness" initiatives
- Sponsoring conferences your ICP doesn't attend
- Expensive website redesigns (a simple, clear site is fine)
- SEO for keywords your ICP isn't searching

The rule of thumb: If you're under $5M in revenue and you don't have 20+ ICP customers yet, spend 90% of your growth budget on sales activities and 10% on supporting marketing (business cards, a decent website, LinkedIn presence). That's it.

As you scale past $5M, you can start shifting the balance. But sales always stays the primary driver.

•••

Now What?

Theory doesn't grow your business. Action does. This week, you have three assignments that will shift your pharmacy from hoping for growth to actively creating it.

Action 1: Map Your ICP's Expensive Problem (30 minutes)

Pull out a piece of paper. Write your ICP at the top. You identified this in Chapter 1.

Now answer this question: "What problem costs my ICP the most money or causes the most pain when it goes unsolved?"

Be brutally specific. "They need prescriptions" is not specific enough.

If you're not sure, call three of your current best customers this week.

Ask them: "What problem were you trying to solve when you started working with us? What was that problem costing you before we fixed it?"

Write down their exact words. Don't translate it into pharmacy jargon. Use their language. That's your sales pitch.

Action 2: Build Your First Target List (1 hour)

Block one hour on your calendar. No interruptions. Open a spreadsheet. Create these column headers:

- Company/Organization Name
- Decision-Maker Name
- Title
- Email

- Phone
- LinkedIn Profile
- Specific Pain Point
- Status

Now fill in 25 rows. Twenty-five companies or organizations that fit your ICP profile exactly.

Use LinkedIn. Use association member directories. Use Google. Ask current customers for referrals.

Find the decision-maker's name and contact information. Don't skip this step. "Office Manager at ABC Clinic" is not specific enough. Get a real name.

This list is your sales pipeline. Everything you do next week depends on having this list.

Action 3: Make 5 Direct Sales Contacts This Week

This is non-negotiable. Not posting on social media. Not tweaking your website. Direct outreach to real people on your target list.

Pick your method: personalized email, phone call, LinkedIn message, or in-person introduction at an event.

Use the email script from this chapter. Customize it for each person. Your goal: book a 15-minute discovery call.

Send 5 messages. Track every response in your

spreadsheet. Update the "Status" column.

If you get a response, great. Schedule the call. If you don't, follow up in 3 days with a different angle.

You'll learn more from 5 direct conversations this week than from 5 months of social media posting.

Bonus Assignment: Audit Your Marketing Spend

Pull up last month's expenses. Add up everything you spent on marketing: ads, social media tools, brand consultants, website updates, graphic design.

Now answer these questions:

- How much did I spend on marketing last month?
- How many ICP customers do I currently have?
- How many new ICP customers did that marketing bring in?

If you spent more than $1,000 on marketing and you have fewer than 20 ICP customers, cut your marketing budget by 50% this month. Seriously. Cut it.

Redirect that money to sales activities: attending the conference your ICP goes to, buying a simple CRM, hiring a part-time business development person, or just paying yourself to spend 10 hours a week on direct outreach.

Marketing feels productive because you're "doing something." But sales is what actually brings in revenue.

•••

You've identified your special customer in Chapter 1. You've built a direct sales engine to reach them in Chapter 2.

But here's the constraint that will eventually hit you: growth is capped by how much work your team can handle.

Every new ICP customer means more prescriptions to process, more prior authorizations to manage, more calls to field.

If you want to scale without burning out your team or exploding your payroll, you need to do what every high-growth pharmacy does: automate everything that doesn't require a human brain. That's exactly what we'll show you how to do in the next chapter.

3

Automate Everything

- The Two Paths to Growth
- The Zero-Labor Prescription
- Build Your Unfair Advantage

The Magic of Automation

Meet the Walberg family Pharmacies. For years, they ran a successful group of community pharmacies, but they were stuck on a hamster wheel. Every time their prescription volume grew, they had to hire another technician. When they acquired a new location, their payroll expenses ballooned right alongside their revenue.

Growth was happening, but it was expensive and heavy. More staff meant more interviews, more training, more management headaches, and thinner margins. They were caught in the classic pharmacy trap: scaling by adding more people.

They could feel the squeeze. Reimbursements from PBMs were tightening every quarter, and the cost of good labor was only going up. Their dream of significant, profitable growth felt capped by the sheer operational drag of managing a large and ever-expanding team.

They knew that if they continued on the same path, they would just be running harder and harder to stay in the same place. The business was growing, but so was their stress. Their freedom was shrinking.

The Turning Point

The breaking point came during a weekly management meeting. They were looking at a forecast that showed a 20% increase in script volume over the next year—but the net profit projection was nearly flat. All the new revenue was being eaten up by the cost of the new hires they would need to handle the work.

That's when they stopped asking, "Who can we hire to do this?" and started asking a much more powerful question:

Can a machine do this?

This question changed everything.

The Big Bet

They made a bold, expensive bet. They invested heavily in a robotic dispensing system. It wasn't just a new piece of equipment; it was a fundamental shift in their operating philosophy.

They didn't just buy a robot—they committed to making automation their core competency. They obsessed over the workflow. They tweaked the software. They redesigned their entire fulfillment process around the machine.

They decided that if they couldn't be the cheapest or the biggest pharmacy, they would be the best in the world at automating prescription fulfillment.

The Second Wave: Data Entry

Next, they aimed their new philosophy at the pharmacy's biggest time-sink: prescription data entry. It was a tedious, error-prone task that consumed thousands of hours across their locations.

They found us, and we worked together to implement a system that automated nearly all of it. Prescriptions arrived electronically, and the system did the work—flagging only the exceptions for human review.

The "after" state was stunning:

- Their variable labor cost per prescription plummeted to almost zero.
- Their single biggest expense—human labor—was virtually eliminated from the equation.
- Their pharmacists and technicians were suddenly freed from repetitive, low-value tasks.
- They could now focus on patient consultations, clinical services, and doctor calls that improved outcomes.
- They could finally use their brains and training instead of just their hands.

The New Economics

Walberg Family Pharmacies had transformed its cost structure. It was no longer 100% variable—where every new script added a proportional labor cost. Instead, they had a high fixed cost (the technology) and a tiny, near-zero variable cost.

They had built a machine. And once you have a machine, you just need to feed it more volume.

Their capacity became enormous. They were so hyper-efficient that they could fill prescriptions for a fraction of what it cost other pharmacies.

This unlocked their second brilliant move: they launched a central fill service.

They went to other independent pharmacies in their region and made them an offer they couldn't refuse:

> Focus on your patients. Let us handle your fulfillment. We can do it cheaper, faster, and more accurately than you can in-house.

They weren't just a pharmacy anymore—they were a technology and logistics company that happened to have a pharmacy license.

They scaled to an eight-figure business not by hiring dozens of new people, but by maximizing the output of their machine and leveraging it to serve others.

•••

The Framework: Shifting from People-Powered to Process-Powered

The Walberg story isn't just about buying a cool robot or using AI to automate prescription entry.

It's about a mindset shift.

You must stop thinking like a traditional pharmacy owner and start thinking like a systems engineer.

Your goal:

Build a business that runs on bulletproof processes and powerful technology, not on the heroic, day-to-day efforts of your team.

Here's how to apply this thinking to your pharmacy—no matter your size or budget.

Part 1: Every Task Is an Automation Candidate

Your first job is to question everything.

The most dangerous phrase in business is "we've always done it that way."

Starting today, become obsessed with challenging every repetitive task in your pharmacy.

For one week, make a log. Don't filter anything.

Ask yourself:

- Who sends invoices to your long-term care facilities?
- Who handles prior authorization follow-ups?
- Who inputs new prescriptions?
- Who manages your monthly marketing newsletter?
- Who places the daily drug order with the wholesaler?

Then ask the brutal question:

Why is a human being still doing this in the year 2025?

The answer is almost always habit, not logic.

Assume every single task can and should be automated until proven otherwise. From invoicing to marketing, dispensing to data entry—it's all on the table.

Part 2: Embrace the 80% Solution

This is where most pharmacy owners get stuck. They look for a perfect solution, and when they can't find one, they default back to manual labor.

They say things like:

> "The robot can't handle reconstituted antibiotics."
>
> "The invoicing system can't manage that one weird account."

So what?

The goal isn't perfection. The goal is leverage. If a system can automate 80% of a soul-crushing task, you've just won.

You've freed up 80% of someone's time and mental energy. The remaining 20% can still be handled by humans.

This changes your financial model:

- When a human does a task → 100% variable cost.
- When you automate 80% → mostly fixed cost.

Fixed cost = scale.

The cost to fill 1,000 prescriptions is almost the same as filling 100.

Your volume can grow 10x—but your payroll doesn't.

That's how you build true operating leverage and massive profit.

Part 3: Automation Is About Math

This shift from variable to fixed cost isn't just operational—it's financial rocket fuel.

You're not just running a pharmacy; you're operating an asset.

Let's talk numbers.

The most important metric for business value is EBITDA (Earnings Before Interest, Taxes, Depreciation, and Amortization). Think of it as the pure cash profit from your operations—the number that buyers and banks care about most.

Here's how automation affects it:

When you automate a task, you:

- Decrease labor costs
- Eliminate payroll taxes and benefits
- Push every dollar saved directly to your EBITDA

Then apply the formula:

Business Value = EBITDA × Multiple

Your multiple (3x, 5x, 7x, etc.) reflects the quality and predictability of your earnings.

Chaotic, owner-dependent businesses get low multiples. Automated, systematized businesses get high ones.

Automation = Double Win

Direct EBITDA Growth

Example: You automate tasks and save $100,000 in salaries.

That adds $100,000 to EBITDA.

At a 5x multiple, that's a $500,000 increase in business value.

Multiple Expansion

Automation makes your business more predictable and less dependent on you.

That lower risk earns a higher multiple—say, from 5x to 6x.

Now your same $100,000 in savings is worth $600,000.

Part 4: If You're Not the Best, Automate It

Be brutally honest:

What is the one thing your pharmacy is truly the best at?

- Is it your high-touch customer service?
- Your deep clinical expertise in diabetes management?
- Your unique relationships with local providers?

That's your human zone. Everything else belongs to automation.

You are not the best in the world at:

- Data entry
- Putting pills in bottles
- Sending billing reminders

Those are commodities. They're distractions from your true calling.

Let machines do what machines do best—repetitive, precise tasks—so your people can do what only humans can do: connect, care, and solve complex problems.

•••

Now What?

This isn't a feel-good chapter. It's a call to act.

This week, you have one non-negotiable assignment that will form the foundation of your automated pharmacy.

Your One-Hour Assignment: Map Your Repetitive Tasks

1. Block exactly one hour in your calendar. Label it "CEO Time." Go to a coffee shop or lock your office door. No interruptions.
2. Grab a whiteboard or a large sheet of paper. Draw two columns:
   - Left column: Task
   - Right column: Hours per week
3. List every non-clinical, repetitive task your team does.
   - Dispensing
   - Data entry
   - Invoicing

- Ordering
- Compliance reports
- Payroll
- Social media posting
- Running sales reports

4. Estimate hours per week for each. Be honest. Ask your team if needed.
5. Circle the top three time sinks. Those are your automation targets—the anchors dragging your profitability.

Your work for this week is done. You've just created your Automation Hit List.

Once you begin freeing your team from these repetitive tasks, their roles will fundamentally change.

How do you measure and improve your operations to keep them lean, focused, and scalable? We'll show you how to keep your business simple and ready for the future in the next chapter.

4

Keep It Simple

- Complexity is the enemy of scale.
- No is a strategic weapon.
- Simple scales, complex breaks.

The Assembly Line That Almost Wasn't

Let me tell you about a pharmacy that built something beautiful, and then almost destroyed it by saying yes to too many things.

We'll call them BigRx. They found their special customer early: telehealth companies prescribing compounded lifestyle medications. Weight loss, hormone optimization, longevity treatments. High-margin, high-volume, predictable work.

Their operation was a thing of beauty. It worked like

a modern factory assembly line, but for pharmacy.

Orders flowed in from their telehealth partners electronically, some via API, some through secure portals, some still by fax, it didn't matter. Our bots grabbed every prescription regardless of format and fed them into a single, unified queue. Within 30 minutes, every order was data-entered, verified by a pharmacist, and sent to the compounding lab.

The lab was equally streamlined. Pre-weighed base compounds. Standardized formulations. Color-coded bins. Every technician knew exactly what to do without asking questions. Compound, label, quality check, ship. The entire process, from prescription received to package out the door, took less than four hours.

They were filling thousands of prescriptions per day with a small, focused team. Their cost per prescription was a fraction of what traditional pharmacies could achieve. Their error rate was near zero. Their telehealth partners loved them because they were fast, reliable, and never complained about volume.

BigRx had found the holy grail: a repeatable, profitable formula that scaled.

And then they started to break it.

Death by a Thousand Opportunities

Success attracts opportunity. And opportunity, if you're not careful, kills what made you successful.

It started small. A local physician's office called. They had a patient who needed a compound that wasn't on BigRx's standard menu. Custom peptide blend, unusual concentration. It would require special sourcing, custom calculations, and a pharmacist spending 30 minutes researching stability data.

The owner, Sarah, hesitated. This wasn't their model. But it was just one prescription. How much harm could it do?

She said yes.

Then an investor approached with an opportunity to enter the veterinary compounding market. Huge market, high margins, underserved. It would just mean sourcing different active ingredients, learning veterinary dosing, dealing with different regulations, and training staff on animal medication safety protocols.

Sarah convinced herself this was "smart diversification."

She said yes.

Within six months, their beautiful assembly line started to turn into chaos.

The Complexity Tax

Here's what nobody tells you about adding new products and services: the cost isn't just the direct expense. It's the hidden tax of complexity that slowly destroys everything.

BigRx's compounding lab, which used to operate like a Swiss watch, now had different workflows running simultaneously. Technicians had to constantly switch contexts.

> "Am I making a semaglutide injection, a custom peptide blend, or a veterinary pain cream? Different process for each."

The error rate tripled. Not because the team got worse, but because the cognitive load became crushing. Every prescription required stopping, thinking, confirming which protocol to follow.

Data entry, which used to be fully automated and took under 30 minutes, now took hours. Why? Because each prescription type required different intake forms, different verification steps, different documentation requirements.

The bots we built for their core business. But every non-standard order required manual data entry.

Inventory management became a nightmare. They used to stock 20 core ingredients in bulk. Now they were managing 60+ SKUs, many of which they only used once or twice a month. Capital was tied up in slow-moving inventory. Expiration dates became impossible to track. They started throwing away expensive, unused ingredients.

Staff training, which used to take two weeks, now took two months. New technicians had to learn not one system, but four different systems depending on which order type they were handling. Sarah couldn't hire fast enough to keep up with turnover.

The biggest killer? Decision fatigue.

Every order that didn't fit the standard template required someone to think: "How do we handle this?" That someone was usually Sarah. She went from spending her time on strategy and growth to spending it answering an endless stream of "what should we do about this one?" questions.

The pharmacy that once filled prescriptions in four hours was now taking days for non-standard orders. Partners started complaining. Some left.

The beautiful machine was breaking down. Sarah's eight-figure dream was collapsing under the weight of complexity she'd voluntarily added.

The Brutal Simplification

Sarah finally hit a wall. She was working 80-hour weeks, her team was burned out, and profits were down despite revenue being up. The cost of complexity had consumed all her margin gains.

She called us to see if the bots could handle all the additional non-standard workflows—but really to figure out how to get out of the mess she was in.

We sat down with her data and showed her something stark. When we mapped revenue, margin, and operational cost by product line, the picture was devastating:

- Core compounded lifestyle meds (their original model): 75% of revenue, 90% of profit, consumed 40% of staff time
- Custom physician compounds: 10% of revenue, 2% of profit, consumed 40% of staff time
- Veterinary compounding: 7% of revenue, basically breakeven after complexity costs, consumed 20% of staff time and created constant regulatory headaches

She'd doubled her operational complexity for a little bit more revenue and a net decrease in profitability. The math was brutal and undeniable.

We asked her a simple question: "What would happen if you went back to just doing what you're great at?"

She was terrified. Wouldn't revenue collapse? Wouldn't she lose momentum?

But deep down, she knew the answer. She'd been running from it for six months.

Over the next 60 days, Sarah made the hardest decisions of her career. She systematically shut down everything that wasn't core.

She stopped taking custom physician orders. She referred those doctors to another local compounding pharmacy that specialized in one-off custom work. They were happy to take the business. She exited veterinary compounding. Cleaned out the inventory. Went back to human-only medications. She said no. Again and again and again.

Her staff panicked at first. "We're shrinking the business! We're going backwards!"

But something amazing happened.

Within 30 days, the assembly line came back. Technicians stopped switching contexts. Error rates dropped back to near zero. The four-hour fulfillment cycle returned. Our automation started humming perfectly again, handling 98%+ of her volume.

Sarah stopped spending her days answering "what do we do about this?" questions and started spending them on what actually mattered: deepening relationships with telehealth partners, optimizing the core process, planning the next location. Staff turnover stopped. Morale recovered. People could breathe again.

And the financials? They were great.

Revenue dropped in the first quarter, but profit increased by nearly 30%. The cost savings from eliminating complexity more than made up for the lost revenue. And the core business, freed from distraction, started growing again.

BigRx was back to growth mode, but this time it was healthy, profitable, and sustainable.

They'd learned the most important lesson in scaling: simple scales, complex breaks.

...

The Framework: The Simplicity System

Sarah's story is about being smart about how you grow. Here's the framework for protecting your core while building an eight-figure business.

Part 1: The KISS Principle for Pharmacy

KISS stands for "Keep It Simple, Stupid." It's an engineering principle that dates back to the 1960s, coined by Kelly Johnson, lead engineer at Lockheed's Skunk Works. The idea was radical: systems work best when they're kept simple rather than made complicated.

Johnson's team designed the SR-71 Blackbird, the

fastest jet ever built, using this principle. Fewer parts, fewer failure points, easier to maintain, more reliable in the field.

The same principle applies to your pharmacy.

Every layer of complexity you add creates exponential coordination costs:

- **Product complexity**: Every new SKU you stock multiplies inventory decisions
- **Process complexity**: Every different workflow multiplies training needs and error potential
- **Customer complexity**: Every different customer type multiplies communication overhead and service requirements
- **Technology complexity**: Every system that doesn't integrate creates manual handoffs

The math is unforgiving. If you have two product lines, two different workflows, and two customer types, you don't have 2+2+2 = 6 units of complexity. You have 2×2×2 = 8 units of complexity, because everything interacts with everything else.

Add a third product line and you're at 3×2×2 = 12.

Add a third workflow and you're at 3×3×2 = 18.

The complexity explodes geometrically while your ability to manage it grows only linearly.

The goal: minimize the variables in your system.

BigRx succeeded when they had:

- **One customer type** (telehealth companies)
- **One product category** (compounded lifestyle meds)
- **One fulfillment process** (standardized assembly line)
- **One intake system** (all orders flow through the same automation)

One, one, one, one. That's 1×1×1×1 = 1 unit of complexity. Easy to train, easy to scale, easy to automate, hard to break.

Part 2: The 80/20 Rule, Weaponized

You've probably heard of the 80/20 rule. It states that 80% of your results come from 20% of your efforts.

But most pharmacy owners don't weaponize it. They acknowledge it intellectually and then ignore it operationally. Sarah certainly did.

Here's how to actually use it:

Step 1: Run your profitability analysis by segment

Create a simple spreadsheet with these columns:

- Product/Service Line
- Monthly Revenue
- Monthly Gross Profit (Revenue minus direct costs)
- Staff Hours Required
- Profit per Staff Hour

Sort by "Profit per Staff Hour" descending.

What you'll find is shocking.

Usually, one or two offerings drive 80%+ of your profit while consuming only 20-40% of your operational resources. Everything else is noise.

BigRx discovered that their core lifestyle compounds generated $400 profit per staff hour. Their custom physician work generated $50 profit per staff hour.

They were subsidizing low-value work with high-value resources.

Step 2: Kill the bottom 20%

This is where most owners freeze. "But we can't just stop offering that service!"

Yes, you can. And you must.

The bottom 20% of your offerings, ranked by profit per staff hour, are actively destroying your ability to scale the top 80%. They're consuming management attention, creating operational friction, and preventing you from achieving the focus required for excellence.

Draw a line. Everything below that line gets sunset over the next 90 days.

Step 3: Double down on the top 20%

Once you've cleared the deadwood, redirect those resources to your highest-value work. The staff hours you were wasting on low-margin custom orders? Now they go toward filling more high-margin core prescriptions.

The capital tied up in slow-moving specialty inventory? Now it goes toward deeper stock of your fast-moving core products, eliminating stockouts and enabling volume discounts.

This is how you get the compounding effect. Simplification creates capacity. Capacity enables volume growth. Volume growth improves unit economics. Better unit economics fund more automation and better systems. The flywheel accelerates.

Part 3: The Strategic "No"

Saying no is hard. Especially when opportunity looks attractive.

But here's the truth: every yes to something outside your core is a no to something inside your core. You only have finite resources, time, attention, capital, and operational capacity.

The question isn't "Can we do this?" The question is "Should we do this instead of doubling down on what's working?"

Sarah's mistake with vet compounding wasn't that vet compounding is bad business. It's that it wasn't her business. It required different expertise, different equipment, different processes. Every hour her team spent on it was an hour not spent perfecting their core compound fulfillment.

The Strategic "No" Framework:

When an opportunity presents itself, run it through this filter:

Question 1: Does this use the exact same operational infrastructure we already have?

- If yes → consider it
- If no → default to no

Question 2: Does this serve the exact same customer profile we already serve?

- If yes → consider it
- If no → default to no

Question 3: Can we become the best in our market at this within 12 months?

- If yes → consider it
- If no → default to no

Question 4: Will this make our core operation simpler or more complex?

- If simpler → consider it
- If more complex → default to no

You need four "yes" answers to proceed. Three out of four is a no. Two out of four is a hard no.

Let's apply this to Sarah's decisions.

Custom physician compounds:

- Same infrastructure? Partially (same lab, but different workflow) → Maybe
- Same customer? No (physicians vs. telehealth companies) → No
- Best in market within 12 months? No (others

specialize in this) → No

- Simpler or more complex? More complex → No

Score: 0 out of 4. Should have been an automatic no.

When you have a clear framework, saying no becomes easy. It's not personal. It's not about being afraid. It's about being strategic.

Part 4: Scaling Through Depth, Not Breadth

There's a common misconception that growth means doing more things. That's breadth. It's seductive because it feels like progress.

Real scale comes from depth: doing one thing so well, so efficiently, so reliably that you can do it at massive volume with industry-leading margins.

BigRx's path to eight figures didn't require them to offer 50 products. It required them to perfect one category of products and then do more volume than anyone else.

The Depth Strategy has three levels:

Level 1: Process Mastery

Get your core offering down to a science. Document every step. Eliminate every inefficiency. Automate every automatable task. Measure every metric. BigRx got their four-hour fulfillment cycle not by accident, but by obsessive process refinement.

Level 2: Volume Scaling

Once your process is dialed in, focus all your energy on increasing throughput. More orders through the same system. This is where economies of scale kick in. Your fixed costs (facility, equipment, management) stay flat while your revenue grows. BigRx went from hundreds to thousands of prescriptions per day through the same assembly line.

Level 3: Geographic Expansion

Only after you've maxed out your process and volume at one location do you replicate. Open a second facility running the exact same playbook. Then a third. It only works if what you're replicating is simple and proven. BigRx is now planning their second location, not because they've mastered 10 things, but because they've absolutely perfected one thing.

Notice what's not in this strategy: diversification. Adding new products. Chasing new customer types.

That's breadth. And breadth is the enemy of scale.

•••

Now What?

Theory won't simplify your business. Action will. This week, you have three assignments that will cut through the complexity holding you back.

Action 1: The Profitability Autopsy (1 hour)

Block one hour with no interruptions. Pull your financial data from the last quarter.

Create a spreadsheet with these columns:

- Product/Service Category
- Revenue
- Direct Costs (product cost, specific labor, specific overhead)
- Gross Profit
- Estimated Staff Hours Required per Month
- Profit per Staff Hour (Gross Profit ÷ Staff Hours)

Fill in every row. Be brutally honest about staff hours. If something "only takes a few minutes per order" but you do 200 orders per month, that's real time.

Sort by "Profit per Staff Hour." Look at the bottom 25% of that list. Those are your complexity anchors. They're sinking your ship.

Circle them. These are your sunset candidates.

Action 2: The Sunset Plan (30 minutes)

Pick the single worst performer from your profitability analysis. The offering with the lowest profit per staff hour that's outside your core.

Write down:

- **What would happen if we stopped offering this in 90 days?**
- **How would we wind it down?** (Notify customers, stop accepting new orders, fulfill existing commitments, etc.)
- **What would we do with the freed-up capacity?** (More of our core work? Better service for core customers?)

Schedule a meeting with your leadership team for next week. Put "Simplification Strategy" on the agenda. Bring your analysis.

You don't have to pull the trigger today. But you need to start the conversation.

Action 3: Install the Strategic No Framework (Ongoing)

Print out the four-question Strategic No Framework from this chapter. Tape it to your desk, or better yet, program it into your decision-making process.

For the next 30 days, every time someone approaches you with a new opportunity, a new product, a new customer type, anything that would add complexity, run it through the filter before you respond. Force yourself to write down the answers to all four questions. No gut decisions. No impulse yeses.

You'll be shocked how many "opportunities" fail the test. And you'll be grateful you had a framework to protect you from your own optimism.

Bonus Challenge: The One-Thing Focus

If you're feeling brave, try this exercise.

Complete this sentence: "We are the best in our market at ______________________."

If you can't finish that sentence with one clear, specific thing, you have a focus problem. Keep simplifying until you can.

BigRx can say: "We are the best in our market at high-volume fulfillment of compounded lifestyle medications for telehealth companies."

What's your one thing?

•••

You've simplified your operations. You've protected your core. Your machine is running clean and fast.

Now it's time to ask the most important question: How

big can this machine get before it stops working?

That's where we're going next. Chapter 5 will show you how to take your proven, simplified formula and scale it aggressively through reinvestment, smart debt, and acquisition.

Let's double down.

5

Double Down

- Bet big on what already works.
- Think like an investor, not an operator.
- Scale faster through disciplined acquisitions.

The Story: How BigRx Grew 30% Overnight

There's a moment in the life of a pharmacy owner that feels like the finish line. The systems you've painstakingly built are humming along. The niche you carved out is generating consistent, high-margin revenue. You look at the profit and loss statement, and for the first time in a long time, the number at the bottom is big, black, and beautiful. You've made it.

This is the moment you've been working for. The stress starts to fade. You can finally breathe. And the first thought that comes to mind is, "I should take some money out." Buy the bigger house, get that boat, and step away from the business more. You deserve it.

This is the Comfort Trap. And it's the most dangerous place you can be.

You mistake a milestone for the final destination. You start treating your business like an ATM when it has just become a high-performance engine. At the very moment you have a proven formula for success, you take your foot off the gas.

The real question to ask in that moment of success isn't "How much can I take out?" It's "How big can this machine get before it stops working?"

Let's go back to Sarah, the owner of BigRx. She had escaped the day-to-day grind by finding her special customer: telehealth prescribers specializing in obesity care.In a crowded, competitive market for GLP-1 drugs, she managed to build trust and became one of the known, established vendors.

We helped automate her operations. She scaled without adding head count. Her sales playbook was bringing in new telehealth groups on a consistent basis. BigRx was a well-oiled machine, and it was throwing off more cash than Sarah had ever seen. The Comfort Trap was calling her name.

But as she looked at her financials, she started to see them differently. She wasn't just a pharmacist anymore. These days were long gone. She was the chief investor of her own company.

She knew her numbers cold. She knew that every dollar she spent on her sales playbook was bringing in five-ten dollars in profit over the next year. Her business wasn't just a job; it was the best investment she could possibly make.

Organic growth was great, but it was slow. And in a hot market like weight loss, competitors were popping up everywhere. Speed was her greatest strategic advantage.

How could she lock in her lead and build a protective moat around her business? The answer wasn't to find more partners one by one. It was to acquire another pharmacy.

Not just any pharmacy. She needed raw materials, a location and a customer list where she could deploy her proven operating system.

She started scouting. Thirty miles away was Main Street Pharmacy. It was a good, solid community pharmacy.

The owner, Frank, was a great pharmacist who was respected by his patients and local doctors. Main Street Pharmacy wasn't failing; far from it. It was well-run.

But Frank was running the pharmacy that Sarah had been running two years ago. He was focused on traditional dispensing and just started to figure out the B2B side, his technology was a step behind with little automation, and he had a really good operational team, but no dedicated sales staff. He was doing well, but he had hit a plateau.

Sarah approached Frank not as a competitor, but as a peer. She laid out her vision: to combine his pharmacy's infrastructure with her pharmacy's technology and specialty focus. She offered him a fair price, well above what the business was netting him, and he saw a great exit for himself and a bright future for his staff and patients.

To fund the deal, Sarah didn't do anything exotic. She walked into a local commercial bank. With her rock-solid cash flow and a clear plan for integrating the new business, she secured a standard business loan.

The bank wasn't betting on a fantasy; they were betting on a predictable, proven machine.

The week after the deal closed, Sarah's team went to work. They didn't fire Frank's staff. They upgraded their tools. They installed our automation, trained the team on some of the nuances in the telehealth model, and began repeating the same playbook that made them win.

The result was stunning.

They plugged a brand-new capacity into an existing, well-run machine. In less than 3 months, the combined company's revenue jumped by 30%.

Sarah hadn't just bought another pharmacy; she had multiplied her success by stamping her proven model onto a new asset.

She had escaped the Comfort Trap by doubling down.

•••

The Framework: Your Three Levers for Aggressive Growth

Sarah's story isn't about getting lucky. It's a repeatable model for any owner who has built a successful formula. Once your business is a predictable profit engine, you have three primary levers you can pull to achieve the next level of explosive growth. It's about shifting your mindset from operator to capital allocator.

Lever 1: Reinvesting Profits

This is your primary engine and the simplest way to scale. Every dollar your business generates can either go into your pocket or go back to work for you.

The math is simple. If you take $20,000 out as a bonus, it's worth $20,000 (before taxes). If you reinvest that same $20,000 into a marketing campaign that you know generates a 3x return, it's worth $60,000 to the business.

Reinvest aggressively when you have a predictable, positive ROI.

Don't just guess. Know your numbers. What happens when you put another $5,000 into Google Ads? What's the return on hiring a dedicated salesperson? When you have a proven cause and effect, every dollar of profit should be seen as dry powder, ready to be deployed for a bigger return.

Lever 2: Using Smart Debt

Most owners are rightly terrified of debt. But there is a massive difference between consumer debt and strategic, productive debt.

Using a credit card to cover payroll is a sign of a failing business. Taking out a term loan to acquire a cash-flowing asset is the work of a smart investor.

A business loan, like the one Sarah got, is simply a tool to pull your future success into the present. The bank gave her the money because they could see her existing cash flow would easily cover the payments. She was borrowing against the predictable future cash flow of her proven system.

Use smart debt for major step-change investments with a clear and calculable return:

- Acquiring a competitor.
- Investing in automation or robotics that dramatically lower labor costs.
- Building out a clean room to launch a lucrative

compounding service.

Don't think of it as taking on a liability. Think of it as purchasing speed.

Lever 3: The Acquisition Playbook

Buying another pharmacy is the ultimate way to double down. You are acquiring the two things that are hardest to build from scratch: a physical location and operational capacity.

The secret is to stop looking for "great" pharmacies to buy. You don't want to buy a perfect business; they are overpriced. You want to buy untapped potential. You're looking for an asset that is worth more in your hands than it is in its current owner's hands.

Use this simple scorecard when scouting targets:

Playbook Compatibility

How easily can you "install" your operating system, your software, your workflows, your marketing and sales into this new business? The easier the integration, the faster the return.

Untapped Potential

Where are they weak where you are strong? If they have no marketing, no specialty services, and outdated tech, those aren't problems; those are massive opportunities for you to immediately add value.

Customer Overlap

Do they serve a patient demographic or have prescriber relationships that fit your existing model? An overlapping customer base makes cross-selling your high-value services incredibly effective from day one.

A Motivated Seller

Look for owners who are nearing retirement, experiencing burnout, or simply lack the energy or capital to get to the next level. They are often more focused on a smooth transition for their legacy than squeezing out every last dollar.

Acquisition is your fastest path from a 7-figure pharmacy to an 8-figure enterprise.

•••

Now What?

This week, your job is to stop thinking like a pharmacy manager and start acting like a capital allocator. These three small assignments will change your perspective.

Action 1: Run Your "Reinvestment ROI" Scenario

Look at last quarter's profit number. Take 20% of that figure. Now, ask yourself:

> "If I was forced to reinvest this amount back into the single most effective part of my business, whether that's marketing, technology, or sales, what would be a realistic financial return in the next six months?"

Write the number down. This makes the power of reinvestment real.

Action 2: Scout One Target

Open Google Maps. Identify one independent pharmacy in a 50-mile radius. Spend 15 minutes being a detective. Look at their website. Read their Google reviews. See what services they offer. Does it look like they are running the business of today or the business of ten years ago? The goal isn't to make an offer; it's to train your brain to see hidden opportunities all around you.

Action 3: Make One Phone Call

Find the name of a local business banker or a lender who specializes in SBA loans.

Send a simple email to request a 15-minute introductory call. Your script is simple: "I'm planning for long-term growth and want to educate myself on what the financing environment looks like for business acquisitions right now."

You are not committing to anything. You are simply gathering the intelligence that all serious CEOs have.

•••

Doubling down through acquisition is a big, strategic risk. But winning in this industry also requires taking smaller, smarter risks every single day.

When a new drug category like the GLP-1s exploded, some pharmacies paused, paralyzed by regulatory confusion, while others leaned in and captured a massive opportunity.

Now that you have the playbook for scale, we need to make sure you have the mindset to navigate the risks that come with it.

6

The Asymmetric Bet

- The biggest risk is playing it safe.
- Smart risk has a defined downside and unlimited upside.
- Speed is a competitive moat.

Risk – The Asymmetric Bet

The biggest risk is playing it safe. In a rapidly changing industry, standing still while others move forward isn't conservative — it's a bet that the world will stay the same. It won't.

Smart risk has a defined downside and unlimited upside. You need to know exactly what you can afford to lose, but the potential gain should be exponential, not incremental.

Speed is a competitive moat. When opportunity

knocks, the pharmacies that move fast, even with incomplete information, capture disproportionate returns. Hesitation costs more than mistakes.

The Fork in the Road

December 2024. The FDA announces that GLP-1 drugs are officially off the shortage list.

For compounding pharmacies across the country, this was a seismic moment. For two years, they had been filling a massive gap in the market, compounding semaglutide and tirzepatide for patients who couldn't access the brand-name versions. The telehealth boom had turned weight-loss compounding into a gold rush.

Overnight, that gold rush appeared to be over.

The big telehealth companies immediately pulled back. Legal teams sent memos. Risk departments issued warnings. The message was clear:

> The shortage exemption is gone. Stop compounding GLP-1s immediately or face legal exposure.

Most pharmacies followed suit. They shut down their GLP-1 programs within days. The logic seemed ironclad:

> Why take the risk? The FDA says the shortage is over. Novo Nordisk and Eli Lilly will sue us. We

could lose our licenses. Better to play it safe.

But two pharmacies in our network took very different approaches. And their divergent paths teach us everything we need to know about risk in business.

Pharmacy A: The Retreat

Let's call the first pharmacy SafeScript. They had built a thriving telehealth compounding business. GLP-1s represented nearly 30% of their revenue.

When the FDA announcement hit, their legal counsel was unequivocal: "Shut it down. Now."

The owner, Mark, didn't push back. The risk felt too big — lawsuits, regulatory scrutiny, potential license revocation. The downside was catastrophic.

Within 48 hours, SafeScript stopped accepting new GLP-1 orders. They notified their telehealth partners that they were exiting the space. They began the process of transitioning existing patients off compounded versions.

Mark told himself he was being responsible. Conservative. Smart.

The numbers told a different story.

Within 30 days, SafeScript's prescription volume dropped 42%. Revenue collapsed. The staff they'd hired to handle the growth suddenly had nothing to do. They had to lay off a significant portion of their staff.

The telehealth partners they'd built relationships with over two years? They immediately found other compounding pharmacies to work with. Those relationships, which had taken years to build, evaporated in weeks.

By March 2025, SafeScript was back to pre-GLP-1 revenue levels — but with higher fixed costs and a demoralized team.

They had "played it safe." And it had cost them two years' worth of progress.

Pharmacy B: The Calculated Bet

Now meet RX Compounding. When the same FDA announcement hit, their owner, Lisa, had a very different reaction. She didn't panic. She read the actual FDA guidance. She consulted with her attorney, a specialist in pharmacy law.

She asked a simple question: "What does the law actually say?"

The answer was nuanced. Yes, the shortage exemption was gone. But the law still allowed compounding when a prescriber determined that an individual patient had a specific medical need that couldn't be met with the commercially available product.

The demand for GLP-1s hadn't disappeared. Millions of patients still couldn't access Wegovy or Zepbound.

Insurance coverage was spotty. Supply was still constrained. The clinical need was real.

Lisa saw something most others missed: this wasn't a shutdown moment. This was a shakeout.

Most pharmacies would retreat. That meant the patients would flood toward the few pharmacies brave enough to stay in the market. This was a massive opportunity disguised as a crisis.

But Lisa wasn't reckless. She built guardrails:

Legal Compliance Framework

She worked with her attorney to create strict protocols. Every prescription required explicit documentation of medical necessity. Every patient needed an individualized assessment from their prescriber. No more bulk telehealth orders without proper clinical justification.

Risk Budget

She calculated exactly what the downside looked like. Worst case: she'd receive a warning letter from the FDA, have to shut down the program, and lose the revenue. She could survive that. She had other revenue streams. The pharmacy wouldn't close.

Upside Assessment

Best case: she'd capture massive market share from competitors who fled. She'd build deep loyalty with prescribers who had nowhere else to turn. She'd establish herself as a trusted provider when others were running scared.

The math was compelling. The downside was survivable. The upside was exponential.

She made the call: "We stay in."

The Asymmetric Payoff

What happened next was stunning.

In January 2025, as SafeScript and dozens of other pharmacies exited, RX Compounding's phones exploded. Prescribers who'd lost their pharmacy partners were desperate. Patients who'd been abruptly cut off were frantic.

Lisa's team worked around the clock. They onboarded new telehealth partners. They processed applications. They documented everything meticulously. By February, their GLP-1 volume had doubled. By March, it had tripled.

Revenue didn't just recover from the brief dip in December — it skyrocketed. They hired aggressively. They expanded their compounding lab. They automated even more of their workflows to handle the surge.

Some competitors who stayed in the market did face legal challenges. Novo Nordisk and Eli Lilly filed lawsuits against a handful of compounding pharmacies. But here's what's crucial: the pharmacies with proper protocols and documentation won their cases.

The lawsuits weren't about whether compounding was legal — they were about whether it was being done properly.

RX Compounding was never sued. Why? Because Lisa had done the work upfront. Her documentation was bulletproof. Her clinical justifications were rock-solid. She had taken a calculated risk, not a reckless gamble.

By mid-2025, as the dust settled, other pharmacies started returning to the GLP-1 market. They'd realized the sky hadn't fallen. But the volume had already shifted. The prescribers had already found new partners. The market share had already been redistributed.

The pharmacies that had fled in December were now fighting for scraps. RX Compounding had won the battle by refusing to retreat.

The final scorecard:

- **SafeScript**: Revenue down 40%, layoffs, damaged relationships, back to square one.
- **RX Compounding**: Revenue up 300%, expanded

> operations, cemented market position, built a defensive moat.

Same moment. Same external shock. Two radically different outcomes.

The difference wasn't luck. It was how they thought about risk.

•••

The Framework: The Asymmetric Risk System

Jeff Bezos has a framework for thinking about risk that every pharmacy owner needs to internalize:

> "Outsized returns often come from betting against conventional wisdom, and conventional wisdom is usually right. Given a 10 percent chance of a 100 times payoff, you should take that bet every time. But you're still going to be wrong nine times out of ten."

Let's break this down into a practical system you can use.

Part 1: Conventional Wisdom Is Usually Right (But Not Always)

When the FDA made its announcement, conventional

wisdom said: "Get out. The risk is too high."

For most pharmacies, that was the right call. If you didn't have strong financial reserves to weather a potential legal issue, exiting was smart. The risk was too high for a poorly prepared pharmacy.

But conventional wisdom has a blind spot: it assumes everyone is in the same position with the same capabilities.

Lisa wasn't in the same position as most pharmacies.

She had:

- **The operational capacity to handle increased volume**
- **Financial reserves to weather a potential shutdown or legal issue**

For her, the conventional wisdom didn't apply. The risk profile was completely different.

The lesson: Question whether conventional wisdom applies to your specific situation.

When everyone is moving in the same direction, ask: "Am I really in the same position as everyone else? Do I have capabilities or resources that change the equation?"

Part 2: Define the Downside First

Most pharmacy owners think about opportunity backwards. They see a potential upside and immediately start imagining success. Then fear creeps in and they freeze.

The right sequence is the opposite: define the downside first. Make it concrete and real.

Lisa didn't start by imagining how much money she could make from GLP-1s. She started by asking:

What's the worst that can happen, and can I survive it?

Her downside analysis looked like this:

Worst-case scenario:

- Receive an FDA warning letter
- Have to shut down GLP-1 compounding immediately
- Lose 60% of revenue within 30 days
- Potential legal fees: $50,000–$100,000

Could she survive that? Yes. She had:

- 6 months of operating expenses in reserve
- Other revenue streams (retail and other compounded meds) that would keep the business

afloat

- The ability to cut costs quickly if needed

The downside was painful but survivable. Once she knew that, the fear lost its power.

The Downside Framework:

When evaluating any major risk, complete this sentence:

> The worst realistic outcome is ______, and if that happens, I will ____________________.

Be specific. Not "I could lose everything" (that's catastrophizing). But:

> "I could lose $200K in revenue over 6 months and another $100K in legal fees, and if that happens, I will cut staff by 2 FTEs, reduce my own salary by 30%, and draw on my line of credit."

If you can articulate a specific, survivable downside, you can move forward. If you can't, the risk is probably too big for your current position.

Part 3: The Asymmetric Upside Test

Here's where most pharmacy owners make a fatal mistake: they take big risks for small gains. They'll stress for weeks about whether to switch to a new wholesaler that might save 2% on cost of goods. But they won't consider a bold move that could 3x their business.

This is backwards.

You should only take significant risk when the potential upside is asymmetric — something vastly larger than the downside.

Bezos again:

> "In business, every once in a while, when you step up to the plate, you can score 1,000 runs. This long-tailed distribution of returns is why it's important to be bold. Big winners pay for so many experiments."

Lisa's GLP-1 bet had asymmetric upside:

- **Downside**: Lose 60% of revenue, potentially face $100K in legal costs
- **Upside**: Triple revenue, dominate market share, build a 5-year competitive moat

The potential gain was 30x the potential loss. That's asymmetric. That's worth the risk.

The Asymmetric Upside Test:

Before taking a major risk, answer these questions:

Is the potential upside at least 5x the potential downside?

- If yes → worth considering

- If no → probably not worth the stress

If this works, does it fundamentally change the trajectory of my business?

- If yes → this is strategic, not just incremental
- If no → save your risk budget for something bigger

Is the upside defensible, or will competitors quickly copy it?

- If defensible → you're building a moat
- If easily copied → the advantage will be short-lived

Lisa's GLP-1 bet passed all three tests. SafeScript's decision to retreat failed all three.

Part 4: Speed Is a Weapon

There's a hidden dimension to risk that most owners miss: the cost of hesitation.

In December 2024, there was a brief window, maybe 2-3 weeks, when the GLP-1 market was in chaos. Prescribers were panicking. Patients were desperate. Pharmacies were making rushed decisions.

Lisa moved fast. Within 72 hours of the FDA announcement, she had:

- Consulted an attorney
- Built her compliance protocols

- Communicated her decision to staff and partners
- Started accepting new orders

By the time most pharmacies were still "evaluating their options," she'd already captured market share.

Speed is a competitive advantage that compounds. The first pharmacy to solve a problem builds relationships, captures volume, and establishes trust. The second pharmacy to solve the same problem has to fight for scraps.

The Speed Framework:

When a major opportunity or disruption hits, you have three options:

- **Move fast with incomplete information** (high risk, high reward)
- **Move deliberately after careful analysis** (moderate risk, moderate reward)
- **Wait and see what others do** (low risk, low reward)

Most owners default to option 3. They're so afraid of making a mistake that they wait for certainty. But by the time certainty arrives, the opportunity is gone.

Lisa chose option 1. She didn't have perfect information. She didn't know if the FDA would crack down harder. She didn't know if she'd face lawsuits. But she had enough information to act. And acting first gave her an insurmountable advantage.

The 72-Hour Rule:

When a major opportunity appears, give yourself 72 hours to make a decision. Not 72 days. Not "when we have more clarity." Seventy-two hours.

Gather the critical information. Consult the right experts. Define your downside. Assess the upside. Then decide.

Bias toward action. You can course-correct later. But you can't recapture lost time.

Part 5: The Risk Portfolio

Here's the final piece of the framework: Not every bet needs to work. You just need one big winner.

Bezos again:

> "We all know that if you swing for the fences, you're going to strike out a lot, but you're also going to hit some home runs."

Lisa didn't just bet on GLP-1s. Over the previous five years, she'd made a dozen bold moves:

- **Launched a telehealth partnership** (worked)
- **Tried veterinary compounding** (failed, exited after 6 months with loss)
- **Invested in AI data entry automation** (worked)

- **Experimented with at-home lab testing** (failed)
- **Built a specialty fertility program** (failed - but broke even)
- **Partnered with a medical spa** (moderate success)

Not every bet paid off. But the ones that worked more than covered the ones that didn't.

This is the power of the risk portfolio approach. You don't need a 100% success rate. You need a portfolio of calculated bets where the winners are so big they dwarf the losers.

Your risk budget:

Allocate 10-20% of your operational capacity (time, capital, attention) to experimentation and calculated risks. Not 100%, that's reckless. But not 0%, that's stagnation.

Think of it as an R&D budget for your business. Some experiments will fail. That's fine. You're buying lottery tickets with positive expected value.

•••

Now What?

Risk isn't theoretical. This week, you're going to practice evaluating and taking smart risks in your business.

Action 1: The Risk Audit (30 minutes)

Pull out a piece of paper. Write down three significant decisions you've been avoiding or delaying in your business. Examples:

- Hiring a key person
- Investing in expensive automation
- Entering a new service line
- Acquiring a competitor
- Switching to a controversial but lucrative drug category

For each one, complete the Downside Framework:

> The worst realistic outcome is ______, and if that happens, I will ____________________.

Be brutally specific. If you can articulate a survivable downside, circle that item. It's worth reconsidering.

Action 2: The Asymmetric Upside Test (20 minutes)

Take the items you circled in Action 1. For each, answer:

- Is the potential upside at least 5x the potential downside?
- If this works, does it fundamentally change my business trajectory?

- Is the advantage defensible for at least 2-3 years?

If you get three "yes" answers, you've found an asymmetric bet worth taking.

Pick one. Just one. You're going to move forward on it this month.

Action 3: The 72-Hour Decision (Ongoing)

The next time a major opportunity presents itself, a potential acquisition, a new partnership, a market disruption, whatever - commit to making a decision within 72 hours.

Set a timer. Block time on your calendar. Gather the essential information. Consult the right experts. Define your downside. Assess your upside.

Then decide.

Action beats perfection. Speed is a moat. Hesitation is expensive.

Bonus Challenge: The Failed Experiment Inventory

This one's uncomfortable, but powerful.

Write down three bold moves you made in the past five years that failed. Bets that didn't work out. Money you lost. Initiatives you shut down.

Now ask: "What did I learn? How did that failure

make me better?"

You'll realize two things:

- The failures weren't as catastrophic as they felt at the time
- You learned more from the failures than the easy wins

This exercise rewires your brain. Failure becomes feedback, not defeat. And you become more willing to take the next smart risk.

•••

You've learned to take smart risks. You've built a culture of experimentation.

But here's the next challenge: as your business grows, you become the bottleneck.

The fastest way to kill momentum is to require your approval for every decision.

In the next chapter, we'll show you how to hire superstars and actually let them run, so your business can scale beyond your personal capacity to manage every detail.

7

Hire Superstars & Let Them Run

- Your biggest bottleneck is you.
- Superstars need three things: clarity, authority, and trust.
- Delegation multiplies. Micromanagement divides.

The Tale of Two Pharmacies

Meet two pharmacy owners who both had the same problem: they were drowning in decisions. Every vendor call, every scheduling conflict, every workflow question ran through them. They were both working 70-hour weeks, and their businesses had plateaued.

They both decided to hire someone talented to take operations off their plate. They both found promising candidates. But what happened next was completely different — and it determined the trajectory of their businesses for years to come.

Riverside Pharmacy: Building a Team of Owners

David owned Riverside Pharmacy, a growing independent that had hit $3M in revenue but couldn't seem to break through. He was the bottleneck. Every decision, big or small, required his approval.

He knew he needed help, but he was terrified of hiring the wrong person. Operations were complex. The economics were razor-thin. One bad hire could be catastrophic.

Then he met Jessica at a local pharmacy conference. She had just graduated from a strong undergraduate business program and had worked as a pharmacy technician throughout college to pay her tuition. She was sharp, asked great questions, and had an intensity about her that was hard to ignore.

David made her an offer: a market-level competitive salary with clear upside if she could help him scale. Jessica accepted.

The Impossible Task

Two weeks into the job, David was explaining one of the pharmacy's biggest operational headaches: the Generic Compliance Ratio problem.

Here's the issue: generics are drastically cheaper when bought from secondary wholesalers. A bottle that costs $23 from a secondary might cost $100 from a primary wholesaler like McKesson, Cardinal, or AmerisourceBergen.

But here's the catch — brand-name drugs are only available through the primary wholesalers. To maintain good pricing and rebates with the primary wholesaler, you need to hit a minimum Generic Compliance Ratio (GCR), a percentage of your generic purchases that must come through them, not the secondary market.

Miss your GCR target, and you lose access to better pricing and rebates. But buy too many generics from the primary, and you're hemorrhaging money on products you could get for a quarter of the price elsewhere.

It was a constant optimization puzzle. David had been doing it himself for years, manually comparing prices, calculating ratios, and placing orders. It took him hours every week and drove him crazy.

Jessica listened carefully. Then she asked, "Can I take a crack at this?"

David's gut instinct was to say, "Let me show you

how I do it first." But something stopped him.

He handed her the login credentials and said, "Figure it out. Let me know if you need help."

The Transformation

Jessica disappeared into the problem. She built a simple spreadsheet that tracked their GCR in real time. She set up alerts so she'd know exactly when they were approaching the minimum threshold. She documented the decision-making process — when to buy from primary, when to buy from secondary, and how to balance cost savings with compliance.

Within a month, she had turned David's chaotic, gut-feel process into a repeatable system. Not only that, she had optimized it. She found $40,000 in annual savings by buying smarter.

David was stunned. Jessica hadn't just learned the process. She had made it better.

That's when David made the most important decision of his business career. He sat down with Jessica and redefined her role entirely, focusing on three different areas:

Clarity:

> "You own all pharmacy purchasing and inventory. Your job is to ensure we never run out

of critical drugs, we hit our GCR targets, and we minimize our cost of goods sold. I don't care how you do it, just hit those outcomes."

Authority:

"You can make any purchasing decision without asking me. If it's over $5,000 for a single order or affects patient safety, give me a heads-up. Otherwise, it's your call."

Trust:

"You're going to make mistakes. That's fine. I made plenty when I was figuring this out. Just learn from them and keep getting better."

Jessica thrived.

Over the next year, she didn't just manage purchasing — she scaled herself. She trained two other technicians on her GCR process, documented everything in a shared manual, and handed off the day-to-day ordering entirely.

She freed herself up to tackle the next operational challenge.

When we arrived to implement our automation and bots at Riverside, Jessica was the point person. She understood the workflows cold. She made fast decisions about how to deal with faxes, which prescriptions to prioritize, and how to structure operations.

When questions came up, she didn't say, "Let me ask David." She said, "Here's what we're doing."

The implementation took three weeks. It finished ahead of schedule and on budget. Jessica's team adopted the new system immediately because she had trained them to think like owners.

David's role transformed. He stepped out of operations entirely and focused on what only he could do: opening a second location, building partnerships with local clinics, and planning the next phase of growth.

Riverside Pharmacy doubled revenue to $6M in 18 months.

•••

Oakwood Pharmacy: The Bottleneck That Never Broke

Now meet Tom, owner of Oakwood Pharmacy.

His story started almost identically. His business was stuck at $2.5M, and he was buried in decisions. He needed operational help.

He hired Michelle, a pharmacy technician with solid experience and great references. On paper, she was perfect.

But Tom couldn't let go.

The Pattern

Michelle would come to Tom with a proposal — a new vendor, a workflow change, a scheduling adjustment. Tom would say, "Let me think about it," or "Send me the details and I'll review."

Michelle would research secondary wholesalers to save money on generics. Tom would redo the analysis himself because "he needed to understand it."

Michelle wanted to adjust staffing to handle the afternoon rush more efficiently. Tom insisted on personally approving the schedule every week.

Michelle quickly learned the unspoken rule: nothing happens without Tom's approval.

Soon, her team learned the same lesson. Every decision became a game of telephone, with every question funneled through Tom. The business stayed stuck.

The Breaking Point

When we arrived to implement our AI automation system, the problems became impossible to ignore.

We needed to configure the voice AI system — a simple decision tree for how the system would route incoming calls. Should refill requests go to option 1 or option 2? Should prescription transfers be option 3 or option 4?

Michelle couldn't decide. She said, "Let me ask Tom what he wants."

But Tom was too busy to sit in the planning meetings. Every question turned into an email thread. Simple decisions, like which number to use for incoming phone calls, took three days to resolve because we were waiting for Tom's input.

Michelle grew frustrated. Our team grew frustrated. The four-week implementation stretched to six weeks.

Worse, the system didn't get fully adopted. Michelle's team didn't feel ownership over the new workflows because they hadn't been empowered to shape them.

They were just following orders. Orders that came slowly and often changed because Tom kept second-guessing decisions.

Six months later, Michelle left. She took a job at a competitor who, in her words, "actually let her do her job."

Tom hired a replacement, but the same pattern repeated.

Today, Oakwood Pharmacy is still around $2.5M in revenue. Tom is still working 70-hour weeks. He's still the bottleneck.

•••

The Framework: The Three-Part Delegation System

The difference between David and Tom isn't luck. It's not even about hiring the "right" person. Both Jessica and Michelle were talented.

The difference is a system.

David built a system that turned talented people into superstars who multiplied his impact. Tom built a system that unintentionally turned talented people into order-takers who waited for permission.

Here's the framework that separates the two.

Part 1: Clarity — Define Outcomes, Not Tasks

Most owners fail at delegation because they confuse telling someone what to do with empowering them to own a result.

Bad delegation sounds like this:

- "Check the Generic Compliance Ratio every Monday and send me the numbers."
- "Order from secondary wholesalers when the price is 30% lower."
- "Ask me before you change anything in the

schedule."

This is a task assignment. You're treating your employee like a pair of hands, not a brain.

Good delegation sounds like this:

- "Your job is to ensure we hit our GCR targets every month while minimizing our cost of goods sold. I don't care how you do it."
- "You own technician scheduling. Make sure we're always properly staffed and labor costs stay under 22% of revenue."
- "Your goal is to reduce our average prescription turnaround time by 20% in the next 90 days without sacrificing accuracy. Figure out what needs to change."

The key difference: you define success by the outcome, not the method. When you give someone a clear outcome to own, you unlock their creativity and intelligence.

Jessica's spreadsheet system wasn't David's idea — it was hers — because she owned the outcome.

Tom never got that innovation from Michelle because he only assigned tasks.

How to apply this in your pharmacy:

Identify your biggest operational headache. Is it inventory management? Staffing? Prior authorizations? Workflow bottlenecks?

Turn it into an outcome. Instead of "manage inventory," say: "Ensure we never run out of fast-moving drugs and we minimize waste from expired inventory."

Hand it to someone talented and step back. Let them figure out how.

Your job is to define success, not prescribe the path.

Part 2: Authority — Set Guardrails, Then Get Out of the Way

Delegation without authority is just glorified task assignment. Your superstar needs real power to make decisions, or they'll constantly wait for your permission and you'll stay the bottleneck.

Here's the simple authority framework David used at Riverside Pharmacy:

The Dollar Threshold

- **Under $2,000**: No approval needed. Just do it and let me know what you did.
- **$2,000–$5,000**: Send me a quick heads-up before you execute. I won't block you unless something's clearly wrong.
- **Over $5,000**: Let's discuss it together and decide.

The Safety Guardrails

- **Patient safety issues**: Immediate escalation to me. No exceptions.
- **Legal or regulatory concerns**: Loop me in before taking action.
- **Anything that could harm our reputation with doctors or patients**: Let's talk first.

The Reporting Rhythm

- **Weekly 15-minute check-in**: What's working? What's not? What help do you need?
- **Monthly review**: Are we hitting our targets? What should we adjust?

Everything else? They decide. No permission needed.

This framework does something magical: it makes your employee think like an owner.

Responsibility creates ownership. Ownership creates results.

How to implement this in your pharmacy:

Sit down with your top performer this week. Use this exact script:

> "I hired you because you're talented. But I've been holding you back by requiring my approval for too many things. That changes today.
>
> Here's what you now own: [describe the

outcome clearly].

Here's your authority: you can make decisions up to $[X] without asking me. For patient safety, legal issues, or anything over $[Y], loop me in. Everything else is your call. I trust you."

Write it down. Make it specific. Make it real.

Part 3: Trust — Embrace Learning Mistakes

Here's the hardest part for most owners: your superstar will make mistakes.

Tom couldn't handle this. Every time Michelle made a small error, Tom would swoop in, fix it himself, and create a new approval process to "prevent it from happening again."

Each mistake led to less trust and more control. Michelle stopped taking risks. She stopped proposing ideas. She just waited for instructions.

David took the opposite approach.

When Jessica made a purchasing mistake — she over-ordered a generic that ended up getting a price drop the next week, costing the pharmacy $1,500 — David didn't blame her.

He asked, "What did you learn? What will you do differently next time?"

Jessica explained her thinking. David helped her refine her decision-making process. She learned. Her next 20 purchasing decisions saved the pharmacy far more than $1,500.

The Trust Framework:

Separate learning mistakes from reckless mistakes.

- **Learning mistake**: "I tried a new vendor and the delivery was late. We won't use them again." → Debrief and improve.
- **Reckless mistake**: "I ignored our inventory alerts and we ran out of critical medication." → Serious conversation.

Most mistakes are learning mistakes. Treat them as tuition for building a better employee. Protect your superstars from low-stakes failure.

If a decision is reversible and the cost is low, let them try it and learn. David's rule: "If it won't cost more than $2,000 to fix and doesn't affect patient safety, just make the call."

Publicly back their authority.

When a technician complained to David about a schedule change Jessica made, David's response was: "Jessica makes those decisions. If you have concerns, talk to her, not me."

This signaled to the entire team: Jessica has real authority. She's not just relaying David's decisions — she's making them.

Tom undermined Michelle constantly. The message was clear: Michelle's authority was fake.

The Multiplication Effect

Here's the secret David discovered: great people hire great people, and empowered people empower others.

Once Jessica felt trusted and empowered, she built a team in her image. She hired two technicians and gave them ownership over specific areas — one owned inventory counts and expiration tracking, the other owned prior authorization follow-ups.

She gave them the same clarity, authority, and trust David gave her. They thrived. They trained others. Jessica had built a team of owners, and each one multiplied David's impact.

Tom built a team of order-takers. They all waited for him. And the business stayed stuck.

•••

Now What?

A framework is useless unless you act on it. This week, you have three assignments that will transform how you lead.

Action 1: The Bottleneck Audit (15 minutes)

Pull out a piece of paper. Write down every decision you made in the past week — from approving a vacation request to choosing a new vendor to deciding how to handle a patient complaint.

Now circle the decisions that only you could make — decisions that require your unique expertise, ownership authority, or external relationships.

Everything else? That's what you should be delegating.

Pick the single biggest time-sink from your "should delegate" list. That's your target for this week.

Action 2: The Authority Conversation (30 minutes)

Schedule a meeting with your highest-performing employee — your Jessica. Block 30 minutes with no interruptions.

Use this script:

> "I want to talk about your role. I hired you because you're excellent, but I've been holding you back by requiring my approval for too many things. That changes today.
>
> Here's what you now own: [describe the outcome clearly: purchasing, scheduling, workflow optimization, whatever you identified in Action 1].

> Here's your authority: You can make any decision under $[choose your number: $1,000, $2,000, $5,000] without asking me. For anything over that, just give me a heads-up before you pull the trigger. If it affects patient safety, legal compliance, or our reputation, loop me in immediately. Everything else is your call.
>
> I trust you. You're going to make mistakes, and that's fine. We'll learn from them together. Go run with this."

Write down the specifics. Give them a copy. Make it real.

Action 3: Practice the Pause (Ongoing)

For the next week, every time an employee asks for your approval on something that should be within their authority — pause.

Don't answer immediately. Instead, ask:

"What do you think we should do?"

Listen to their answer. Let them make the decision. Bite your tongue. Resist the urge to "fix" it unless it clearly violates a safety guardrail or will cause serious harm.

This is uncomfortable. You'll want to jump in. Don't.

This is how you build owners, not employees.

This is how you multiply yourself.

•••

You've hired superstars and given them authority to run. Your operations are humming. But here's the uncomfortable truth: your biggest competitor isn't the pharmacy down the street. It's your own cost structure.

Let's talk about how to win that fight in the next chapter.

8

Competition Is Your Cost

- Your real competitor isn't the pharmacy down the street.
- Obsessing over competitors creates a distraction tax.
- Lower costs create strategic freedom.

The Pharmacy That Couldn't Stop Looking Over Its Shoulder

Let me tell you about a pharmacy that had everything it needed to succeed — except the right focus. BlueRiver Pharmacy, a small independent in Yonkers, New York, filled about 400 scripts a day. Solid location. Loyal patient base. Experienced owner.

But the owner, Frank, was consumed by one thing: the competition.

- Three other pharmacies within a mile radius
- Frank knew their hours, staffing levels, pricing strategies — even their personalities
- He drove past them daily, checking parking lots to see how busy they were

When a competitor ran a promotion, Frank matched it. When another hired a new technician, he worried about poaching. When a third started offering delivery, he scrambled to launch his own service — even though his margins couldn't support it.

Every decision ran through one question: "What are they doing?"

The Paranoia Tax

Frank's obsession created what we call The Paranoia Tax — the hidden cost of fear-based decisions.

He came to us wanting automation. His team was drowning in prescription processing. Data entry alone took 30+ hours a week. The case for automation was obvious: eliminate that workload, free up staff, improve turnaround times.

But Frank had one condition that shocked us: "Don't run the automation on weekends."

Why? A per-diem pharmacist worked weekends — and rotated between nearby competitors.

Frank worried:

- "If he sees how efficient our system is, he'll tell the others."
- "They'll copy us."
- "Or they'll poach my techs."

We explained the logic didn't hold. Competitors could adopt automation anytime. By holding back, Frank kept his Saturday chaos intact. He handicapped his own business to hide from others.

He didn't budge. Weekends stayed manual.

Over the next two years, he layered on more friction:

- **Refused to document workflows** ("If someone leaves, they'll take our secrets.")
- **Avoided investing in software** ("If my techs know the cost, they'll ask for raises.")
- **Filtered every improvement through fear of being copied or exposed**

Result: BlueRiver Pharmacy stagnated.

The Pharmacies That Looked Inward

Two other owners faced the same market, the same challenges — but not the same fate.

Pharmacy A: Hudson Pharmacy

Maria, the owner, had three competitors within two miles. She knew them — but didn't obsess.

When we implemented automation, she ran it seven days a week — full deployment. When her weekend pharmacist asked about it, she showed him."If they want to improve, great. That raises the bar for everyone."

Maria's philosophy: "I can't control what they do. I can only control my costs and my service."

She focused relentlessly on her unit economics —
What does it cost to fill each prescription?
Where are the leaks?

Within 18 months, Hudson Pharmacy had:

- Cut labor cost per prescription by 40% through automation
- Negotiated better terms with secondary wholesalers
- Built a lean, efficient operation that generated healthy margins

Revenue grew 2X.

Profit grew 3X.

When a competitor tried to undercut her, Maria matched prices easily — her margins were strong enough. Six months later, that competitor quietly reversed course.

She didn't win by watching them. She won by mastering her own economics.

Pharmacy B: Beacon Compounding

James faced even heavier competition — dozens of online, venture-backed compounding rivals.

He could have:

- Studied their pricing
- Worried about their marketing
- Tried to out-advertise them

Instead, he focused on operational efficiency.

He automated everything:

- Prescription intake
- Shipping and compounding worksheets
- Patient communication

His goal: become the lowest-cost operator in his market.

And he did. Automation and optimization cut his cost per prescription to one-third of traditional peers.

That created leverage:

- Charge 20% less and still profit
- Or keep prices flat and bank the margin

When a national competitor flooded his region with ads, James didn't flinch. His customers stayed for service and fair prices. His margins let him grow sustainably without chasing every lead.

Two years later, Beacon Compounding grew 3X.

> "I stopped worrying about what they were doing," James said, "and started focusing on what I was spending. That's when everything changed."

The Two-Year Scorecard

BlueRiver Pharmacy (Frank):

- **Revenue**: Flat / slight decline
- **Profit margin**: 8% → 5%
- **Staff turnover**: High
- **Owner mindset**: Burned out, reactive
- **Automation**: 60% (weekends manual)
- **Position**: Weak, barely surviving

Hudson Pharmacy (Maria):

- **Revenue**: 2X growth

- **Profit margin**: 7% → 12%
- **Staff turnover**: Low
- **Owner mindset**: Strategic, calm
- **Automation**: 100%
- **Position**: Strong, building a moat

Beacon Compounding (James):

- **Revenue**: 3X growth
- **Profit margin**: 9% → 15%
- **Staff turnover**: Minimal
- **Owner mindset**: Focused, scaling
- **Automation**: 100%+
- **Position**: Dominant in niche

Same conditions. Same market. Different outcomes. The difference was focus.

Frank focused on them. Maria and James focused on themselves.

•••

The Framework: The Cost-Control Philosophy

Part 1: The Fundamental Truth About Competition

Most owners think the goal is to beat others. It's not. The goal is to stay profitable.

You stay alive by making more than you spend.

Revenue is influenced by factors you can't control:

- PBM rates
- Insurance contracts
- Market demand
- Economy
- Patient preferences
- Competitor actions

But costs are almost fully within your control:

- Hiring and wages
- Tech investments
- Lease vs buy decisions
- Marketing spend
- Inventory levels
- Vendor contracts

Your competitive advantage is cost control. The pharmacy with the healthiest margins wins — always.

Part 2: The Three Questions That Matter

Start filtering decisions through these three questions instead of "What will the competition think?"

1. Does this improve my unit economics?

> wwwCost per prescription = All expenses ÷ Total prescriptions.

Track:

- Labor (pharmacist + tech)
- Product cost
- Supplies
- Overhead

If you're not tracking it, you're flying blind.

Maria knew hers: from $12 → $7 after automation.

2. Does this increase my margin buffer?

A margin buffer buys freedom:

- Survive PBM cuts
- Weather slow months
- Invest in growth

- Underprice when needed
- Say no to bad business

Frank had 5%. James had 15%. One feared losses; the other funded growth.

3. Can I afford this if revenue drops 30%?

The stress test: If the answer's no, the cost is too risky.

Part 3: The Cost-Control Hierarchy

Tier 1 – Variable Costs (Scale with Volume)

- Drug costs
- Packaging
- Per-prescription labor

Goal: drive to zero through automation. Automation converts variable labor into fixed tech costs.

Tier 2 – Fixed Costs (Stay Constant)

- Rent / utilities
- Core salaries
- Software

Goal: minimize without hurting quality. Frank added fixed costs without ROI. Maria didn't.

Tier 3 – Investment Costs (Strengthen Future)

- Automation
- Training
- Equipment upgrades

Goal: invest aggressively when ROI is clear.

Maria paid $45K → saved $150K/year.

James paid $60K → saved $500K over 2 years.

These are the only costs that make you stronger.

Part 4: The "Ignore the Competitor" Framework

When tempted to react to a competitor:

Default: Do nothing. Focus inward.

Only act if:

- Their change fundamentally alters market economics
- Multiple customers explicitly ask for it
- It genuinely improves cost structure

Everything else — ignore it.

Frank matched a "free delivery" offer without analysis. It drained his margin.

The competitor quit months later; Frank didn't.

Part 5: The Abundance Mindset

Stop seeing pharmacy as zero-sum.

Frank believed every competitor's gain was his loss.

Maria and James believed a rising industry lifts all boats.

Maria:

- Shared notes with competitors
- Referred owners to our automation
- Said "If they improve, great — it helps everyone."

James:

- Joined a mastermind group
- Shared what worked and what didn't
- Collaborated on vendor negotiations

They understood: Your competitors aren't your enemies. Your costs are.

Healthy margins breed generosity. Tight margins breed fear.

•••

Now What?

Stop looking over your shoulder. Start looking at your own numbers.

Action 1: Calculate Your Cost Per Prescription (1 hour)

If you don't know this number, you're blind.

Formula:

> Total Operating Expenses ÷ Total Prescriptions Filled

Include:

- Labor (all staff)
- Drug costs
- Overhead (rent, utilities, insurance, software)
- Supplies (vials, labels, bags)

Write it down. That's your baseline.

Ask: "How can I cut this by 20% in 12 months?"

Action 2: The Competitor Distraction Audit (30 minutes)

Pull your calendar. Estimate time spent:

- Checking competitor websites or social media

- Driving past their locations
- Asking staff what they've heard
- Reacting to promotions or changes
- Worrying about what's next

Add it up. That's your Paranoia Tax.

Now ask: "What if I spent those hours improving operations instead?"

Action 3: The 30% Stress Test (30 minutes)

List your top five expenses.

1. ________________________
2. ________________________
3. ________________________
4. ________________________
5. ________________________

Now ask for each: "If revenue drops 30%, can I still afford this?"

If not:

- Can I eliminate it?
- Can I reduce it?
- Can I make it variable?

- Does it lower future costs long-term?

Circle the most fragile expense. That's your target to fix this quarter.

•••

Bonus Challenge: The Abundance Experiment

Reach out to one local competitor. Not to spy — to connect.

Message:

> "Hey, we're both in a tough industry. Want to grab coffee and swap notes on what's working? No pressure."

You'll realize, they're not your enemy. They're another owner fighting the same battle. When you stop seeing them as threats, you stop making fear-based decisions.

That's when you start winning.

•••

You've learned to control costs and build margins. Your business is financially sound.

Next comes speed — the ultimate advantage.

In the next chapter, you'll learn why urgency is the difference between capturing opportunity and watching it pass you by.

9

A Deadline To Keep

– Urgency is a competitive moat.

– Deadlines create clarity and focus.

– Speed attracts talent and opportunity.

The Pharmacy That Moved at the Speed of Now

September 2025. We had just onboarded twenty-three new pharmacies for automation implementation. Our standard timeline was four weeks: Week 1 for discovery and data gathering, Week 2 for system configuration, Week 3 for testing and training, Week 4 for go-live and stabilization.

It was a proven process. Methodical. Low-risk. Most pharmacies appreciated the structure because it gave them time to "get ready."

Then I received an email that changed how I thought about implementation forever.

The subject line: "Let's move faster."

It was from Jake, owner of Art of Care Compounding in Philadelphia. His pharmacy was scheduled to start implementation in six weeks. He wanted in, now.

But it wasn't just impatience. The email was precise:

> "Jonathan – I know your standard process is four weeks, and I respect that. But I'm not like most pharmacies. When we decide to do something, we move quickly. If you can move us to the front of the implementation queue, I guarantee we'll complete this in two weeks, not four.
>
> We've already done our homework. Attached is every piece of information you typically spend Week 1 gathering: our current workflows, our prescription volume breakdown, our software credentials, our team structure, our pain points ranked by priority. Everything.
>
> We're not asking you to cut corners. We're asking you to match our pace. Give us the early slot, and we'll prove that urgency is a multiplier, not a risk."

I opened the attachment. He wasn't bluffing. It was a 15-page document that answered every discovery question we typically spent hours on meetings extracting from new clients. Workflow diagrams.

Screenshots of their systems.

Most pharmacy owners can't tell you the exact steps of entering an order without working through it. Jake had documented his operation down to precise and exact steps.

I called him within an hour.

The Two-Week Blitz

We moved Art of Care to the front of the queue. Not because we were doing them a favor, but because I was genuinely curious: Could this actually work?

Most implementations drag because of one thing: waiting.

- Waiting for the pharmacy to send us login credentials.
- Waiting for them to schedule training time.
- Waiting for decisions on configuration options.
- Waiting for them to "find time" to test the system.

With Art of Care, there was no waiting.

- **Day 1**: We sent the technical requirements checklist at 9 AM. Jake's IT person responded at 11 AM with everything configured.
- **Day 3**: We needed to map their prescription workflow to our automation logic. Most

pharmacies take a week to schedule a 60-minute workflow session. Jake's entire leadership team—pharmacist, lead tech, operations manager—was on a virtual call with us by 2 PM that same day.

- **Day 5**: We delivered the first build of their automation. Most pharmacies take 3-5 days to test it. Jake's team tested it within 6 hours and sent us detailed feedback by end of day.
- **Day 8**: We made the adjustments. They retested. Approved. Hand-off scheduled for the next morning.
- **Day 9**: Hand-off session. We showed their team the new system. Most pharmacies need multiple sessions because staff trickle in and out. Jake had his entire team in one room. Full attendance. No interruptions. They asked sharp questions. They took notes.
- **Day 11**: Go-live. Most pharmacies go live on a Monday to give themselves a full week to troubleshoot. Jake insisted on going live on a Wednesday. "If there are issues, we'll fix them in real-time. Waiting until Monday just delays the benefit."
- **Day 14**: Final check-in. The system was humming. Prescription intake that used to take 30 minutes was now under 5 minutes. Error rates had dropped. The team was thrilled.

Jake was right. Two weeks. Not four. But here's what shocked me even more: his team wasn't stressed. They were energized.

During our final call, I asked Jake's lead technician how she felt about the rapid implementation. I expected her to say it was exhausting.

Instead, she smiled.

> "This is the best two weeks I've had in years. We actually got something done. No endless meetings. No "let's revisit this next week." We made a decision, executed, and moved on. I wish everything in this pharmacy worked like this."

That's when I realized: Urgency isn't stressful. Ambiguity is stressful. Delay is stressful. Urgency, when paired with clarity, is exhilarating.

The System Migration No One Thought Was Possible

Three months later, Jake called me with a new challenge.

Art of Care was outgrowing their pharmacy management system. It was slow, clunky, and couldn't handle their compounding volume. They wanted to migrate to a modern system built for high-volume compounding.

Any pharmacy owner will tell you: switching

pharmacy management systems is a nightmare. It's not just software; it's your entire operational backbone. Patient records. Prescription history. Inventory. Billing. Integrations. One mistake, and you could lose critical data or halt operations entirely.

Most pharmacies talk about switching systems for years. Some never do it. The ones that do typically take 12-24 months from decision to go-live.

Jake's timeline? Three months.

I tried to talk him out of it. "Jake, this isn't like our automation. This is core infrastructure. If something goes wrong, your entire pharmacy shuts down. You need time to plan, test, and phase this carefully."

His response:

> "Jonathan, I appreciate the caution. But we've already mapped out the entire migration plan. We know exactly what data needs to transfer, what workflows need to change, and what risks we're managing. We're not rushing. We're moving with precision. There's a difference."

He was right. Again.

When I asked Jake how they pulled it off, his answer was simple:

"We treated the deadline like it was real."

The Culture of Urgency

Most pharmacies treat deadlines as suggestions. "We'll try to get this done by Q2" becomes Q3, then Q4, then "maybe next year."

Jake's pharmacy operated differently. When they set a deadline, it was sacred.

But here's the key: it wasn't just top-down. The culture of urgency flowed in every direction.

From Jake to his staff:

Every initiative had a clear owner and a specific deadline. Not "let's work on improving our refill process." But: "Sarah, you own refill optimization. The goal is to reduce average refill time from 24 hours to 12 hours. Deadline: March 15. Weekly check-ins every Monday at 9 AM."

From staff to vendors:

When Art of Care's team worked with vendors, they expected the same urgency they operated with. If a vendor promised a response "by end of week," Jake's team would follow up Friday morning. Not to be annoying, but to keep momentum.

From vendors to Art of Care:

Vendors quickly learned that Art of Care was different.

When we sent them a request, they knew a delay would be met with immediate escalation. Not anger. Just: “We need this to stay on schedule. What’s blocking you? How can we help?”

From customers to Art of Care:

Prescribers loved working with them because things moved fast. A new operational workflow that took other pharmacies 3 days? Art of Care handled it in 6 hours. A compounded prescription that normally took 48 hours? They shipped it same-day.

That reputation compounded. Prescribers referred more patients. Patients became loyal. Competitors couldn’t keep up.

The Talent Magnet

Here’s the most surprising outcome of Jake’s urgency culture: it attracted exceptional people.

Most pharmacy owners complain about hiring. “Good people are impossible to find. Everyone just wants a paycheck and doesn’t care about the work.”

Jake didn’t have this problem. Why? Because A-players are allergic to slow-moving organizations. Talented people are frustrated by:

- Endless meetings that go nowhere
- Initiatives that drag on for months without

progress

- Bosses who can't make decisions
- Environments where nothing ever gets done

Jake's pharmacy was the opposite. Things moved. Decisions were made. Projects finished. People saw the impact of their work immediately.

When Jake posted a job opening for a pharmacy technician, he included this line in the description:

> "We move fast here. If you thrive in an environment where things get done, where deadlines are real, and where execution matters, you'll love it. If you prefer a slow, steady pace, we're probably not the right fit."

He got 50 applications. Most were generic. But three stood out. They explicitly mentioned the urgency line. "That's exactly the kind of place I want to work."

Jake hired all three. Two years later, all three were still there, now in leadership roles.

The self-selection effect: By making urgency part of the culture, Jake naturally attracted people who valued urgency. And those people hired others like them.

The result? A team of high performers who held each other accountable. No one wanted to be the person who slowed the team down.

The Valid Reasons for Delay

Now, let's address the elephant in the room: What about when deadlines are missed?

Because they will be. No matter how disciplined your culture, delays happen. The question is: how do you handle them?

Jake's approach was simple and consistent:

1. Every missed deadline required an explanation—immediately.

Not "I'll get to it eventually." Not silence. If a deadline was missed, the person responsible had to communicate why it was missed and when it would be completed. Same day.

2. Valid reasons were accepted without fuss.

- "The vendor didn't deliver the data we needed on time. I've escalated. New deadline: Friday."
- "I underestimated the complexity. This task is 3x bigger than we thought. I need two more days."
- "An urgent patient issue came up that took priority. I'll have this done tomorrow morning."

Jake didn't punish people for valid delays. He just wanted transparency.

3. Invalid reasons were called out—kindly but firmly.

- "I didn't have time." (Translation: I didn't

prioritize it.)

- "I forgot." (Translation: I didn't track it.)
- "I was waiting for you to tell me what to do." (Translation: I didn't take ownership.)

When someone gave an invalid reason, Jake' response was consistent:

> "I get it. We all have competing priorities. But this was important enough to have a deadline. If you couldn't hit it, I needed to know earlier so we could adjust. Let's talk about how to avoid this next time."

No shame. No anger. Just accountability.

4. Repeated delays triggered a deeper conversation.

If someone consistently missed deadlines, Jake didn't ignore it. He sat down with them privately: "I've noticed you've missed the last three deadlines. What's going on? Are you overloaded? Are the deadlines unrealistic? Do you need help? Let's figure this out."

Sometimes the person was in the wrong role. Sometimes they needed training. Sometimes they just needed clearer expectations.

But Jake didn't let delay become normal. He defended the culture of urgency.

•••

The Framework: Building a Culture of Urgency

Jake's pharmacy didn't become fast by accident. It was a system. Here's how to replicate it.

Part 1: The Deadline Mandate

Rule: Every initiative gets a deadline. No exceptions. Not "we'll work on this." Not "let's make progress." Every project, every task, every improvement gets a specific, written deadline.

How to implement:

1. Use the "Who, What, When" format for every assignment.

   Bad: "We need to improve our inventory system."

   Good: "Sarah owns inventory optimization. The goal is to reduce stock-outs by 50%. Deadline: March 30. Weekly check-ins Mondays at 10 AM."

2. Write it down.

Verbal commitments don't count. Put it in an email, a shared document, a project management tool. Make it visible.

3. Default to shorter deadlines.

If you're not sure how long something will take, guess

short. You can always extend. But starting with a tight deadline creates urgency.

Jake's rule: "If I think something will take a month, I set the deadline for three weeks. We almost always hit it."

Part 2: The Daily Standup

Most pharmacies don't have any regular rhythm for accountability. Projects drift because no one's checking in.

Jake's solution borrowed from the tech world: a 10-minute daily async standup. Every afternoon at 4:00 PM, his core team sent a message on their internal communication tool (slack).

The format was rigid:

1. Each person shares (30 seconds max):
    - What I accomplished yesterday
    - What I'm working on today
    - Any blockers or delays
2. Deadlines at risk get flagged immediately.

If someone says, "I'm supposed to finish X by Friday, but I'm not going to make it," the team addresses it right there. Do we push the deadline? Do we reassign? Do we remove a blocker?

3. No problem-solving in the standup.

If an issue requires discussion, Jake would say, "Let's talk about that offline. Sarah and I will meet at 10 AM to sort it out." The standup wasn't a meeting. It was a synchronization ritual.

Ten minutes. Every day. Non-negotiable.

Why it worked:

- **Accountability**: You can't hide when you report daily.
- **Visibility**: Everyone knew what everyone else was working on.
- **Speed**: Blockers got resolved within hours, not weeks.

Part 3: The Escalation Protocol

Urgency dies when problems sit unaddressed. Jake's team had a clear protocol for escalating issues:

1. Level 1: Team member tries to solve it themselves (same day).

Example: A vendor didn't send the expected data. The team member calls the vendor, explains the urgency, and asks for a new timeline.

2. Level 2: If unresolved by end of day, escalate to manager.

The manager steps in with more authority. "This is

holding up our deadline. We need this by noon tomorrow. What can we do to make that happen?"

3. Level 3: If still unresolved, owner gets involved.

Jake rarely had to escalate to this level, but when he did, he moved fast. A single phone call from the owner to the vendor's VP usually unstuck things immediately.

The key principle: Don't let blockers linger.

Part 4: The Retrospective Ritual

Every time a major project finished—whether it hit the deadline or not—Jake's team did a 30-minute retrospective.

Three questions:

- What went well?
- What didn't go well?
- What will we do differently next time?

Example: After the pharmacy system migration, the retrospective revealed that data validation took longer than expected because they didn't test the export format early enough.

Action item: "On future migrations, we test data exports in Week 1, not Week 5."

This ritual did two things:

- It closed the loop. The project wasn't done until the team learned from it.
- It compounded improvements. Each project made the next one faster.

Part 5: The Respect for Rest

Here's the counterintuitive part: Jake's team didn't burn out.

How is that possible? They were moving fast, hitting tight deadlines, operating with constant urgency. Shouldn't they be exhausted?

The secret: Urgency isn't the same as overwork.

Jake's team worked hard during work hours. But when they left, they left. No expectation of answering emails at 10 PM. No guilt about taking time off. No glorification of 80-hour weeks.

Why? Because efficiency eliminates the need for overwork.

When you move fast, when you don't let projects drag, when you execute with precision, you don't need endless hours. You just need focused hours.

Jake's philosophy: "I'd rather have 6 hours of intense, focused execution than 12 hours of distracted, meandering effort."

His team worked 8-9 hour days. They took

vacations. They had boundaries. And they got more done than pharmacies where people worked 60-hour weeks.

Urgency creates efficiency. Efficiency creates margin. Margin creates sustainability.

•••

Now What?

This week, you're going to take three specific actions to build urgency into your culture.

Action 1: The Deadline Audit (30 minutes)

Pull out a piece of paper. List every active project or initiative in your pharmacy right now.

For each one, answer:

- Who owns this?
- What is the specific, measurable outcome?
- What is the deadline?

If you can't answer all three questions for a project, it doesn't have a real deadline. And if it doesn't have a real deadline, it's not going to get done.

Pick the three most important projects.

For each one, write down:

- **Owner** (name, not "the team")
- **Outcome** (specific and measurable)
- **Deadline** (exact date)

Send an email to each owner with their assignment.

Use this exact format:

> "You own [project]. The goal is [specific outcome]. Deadline: [date]. Let's check in weekly on [day] at [time]. Let me know if anything's blocking you."

Action 2: Implement the Daily Standup (Starting Tomorrow)

Tomorrow morning, gather your core team for 10 minutes before you open.

Tell them:

> "We're starting a new ritual. Every morning at [time], we're going to do a quick standup. It'll take 10 minutes max. Each of you will share what you did yesterday, what you're doing today, and any blockers. That's it. No long discussions. Just quick updates."

Do it every day for two weeks. No exceptions. Not

"when we have time." Every. Single. Day.

After two weeks, ask your team: "Is this helpful or annoying?" You'll be surprised. Most will say it's the most valuable 10 minutes of their day.

Optionally - if your team is large, do it via a written format in any of the many communication or project management tools.

Action 3: The Escalation Conversation (This Week)

Schedule a 15-minute meeting with your highest-performing team member.

Ask them: "When you hit a blocker—a vendor delay, a decision you need from me, a dependency on someone else—what do you do?"

Listen to their answer.

Then say:

> "Here's what I want you to do from now on. If something's blocking you, try to solve it yourself that same day. If you can't, escalate to me immediately. Don't wait. Don't let it sit. I'd rather know about a problem today than find out next week that it's been sitting unresolved. Deal?"

This single conversation changes the game. It gives your team permission to move fast and escalate when needed.

Bonus Challenge: The Two-Week Sprint

Pick one project that's been lingering for months. Something you keep saying you'll get to "eventually."

Set a two-week deadline. Commit to finishing it in 10 business days. Why two weeks? Because it's long enough to get real work done, but short enough to maintain urgency.

Tell your team:

> "We're doing a sprint on [project]. Two weeks. That's it. We're going to move fast, make decisions quickly, and get this done. It won't be perfect, but it'll be done."

You'll be amazed what happens when you give yourself a tight, real deadline.

•••

You've built urgency into your culture. You're executing faster than your competition. Your team is energized. Projects are finishing.

But all of this, the customers, the systems, the culture, was built on a foundation of innovation. And that's where we end. In the final chapter, we'll tie it all together and talk about what it really means to forge your own path in an industry that too often rewards conformity over creativity.

10

Forge Your Own Path

Choose Who You're For

The journey starts with clarity. You can't build an eight-figure pharmacy by trying to serve everyone. You need to find your special customer, the one who values what you uniquely offer and is willing to pay for it. That's your ICP. Everything else flows from that decision.

Once you know who you're serving, you need to reach them. Not through hope and brand awareness, but through direct, deliberate sales. Marketing makes you known. Sales makes you money. Build your target list, make direct contact, prove your value with pilots, and systematically close deals. Only after you have a proven sales engine should you layer in marketing to amplify what already works.

Build Systems That Scale

Growth will stress your operations. The only way to scale without drowning your team is to automate relentlessly. Every repetitive task is an automation candidate. Embrace the 80% solution. Transform your cost structure from variable to fixed. Free your people from soul-crushing work so they can focus on what only humans can do.

But automation alone isn't enough. As you grow, complexity will try to kill you. Every new product line, every new customer type, every new workflow multiplies your coordination costs. The path to eight figures isn't doing more things, it's doing fewer things exceptionally well. Protect your core. Say no to distractions.

Simple scales. Complex breaks.

Play Offense When the Math Works

When you find a formula that works, double down. Reinvest your profits. Use smart debt to pull future success into the present. Acquire competitors and stamp your proven playbook onto their assets. The biggest risk isn't betting big on what works. It's staying small when you should be scaling.

Taking smart risks requires a different mindset. Define your downside first. Make it concrete and survivable. Then assess if the upside is asymmetric, at least 5x the potential loss. When the math works and the window is open, move fast.

Speed is a competitive moat.

Hesitation costs more than mistakes.

Your growth will eventually outpace your personal capacity. The only solution is to hire superstars and actually let them run. Give them clarity on outcomes, authority to make decisions, and trust to learn from mistakes. Delegation multiplies your impact. Micromanagement divides it. Build a team of owners, not order-takers.

Build a Business That Runs Without You

As you build, ignore the noise. Your real competitor isn't the pharmacy down the street. It's your own cost structure. Obsessing over what others are doing is a distraction tax. Focus inward. Control what you can control: your unit economics, your margin buffer, your operational efficiency.

Lower costs create strategic freedom.

Finally, operate with urgency. Every initiative needs a deadline. Every project needs an owner. Every blocker needs immediate escalation. Urgency isn't stressful when paired with clarity. Ambiguity and delay are what burn people out. Speed becomes a self-fulfilling prophecy: it attracts talent, compounds results, and creates momentum that competitors can't match.

This is the playbook that built eight-figure pharmacies across every segment of the industry. Community, specialty, compounding, long-term care, digital. The specifics varied, but the principles held.

•••

This Is Just Our Roadmap

But here's what I need you to understand: This is just our roadmap. It's not the only road.

Every pharmacy we've worked with that achieved extraordinary success did something we didn't expect. They took the principles we shared and bent them in ways we hadn't imagined. They experimented. They tried things that seemed crazy. Some failed. Some worked spectacularly.

- One owner built a thriving pharmacy by partnering exclusively with funeral homes.
- Another found their niche serving traveling nurses in remote locations.
- A third became the go-to pharmacy for a specific

genetic disorder so rare that most pharmacists had never heard of it.

None of these models came from a textbook. They came from someone willing to forge their own path.

The core of innovation isn't following a formula. It's experimenting with new ideas and seeing what works. You're going to face decisions we never covered. Markets we've never seen. Opportunities that don't fit neatly into any framework. And in those moments, you'll have to trust yourself to figure it out.

Some of the ideas we presented will be directly applicable to your business. Use them. Others won't fit. Ignore them. And some will need to be adapted, twisted, or completely reimagined to work in your specific context. Do that.

The pharmacies that win aren't the ones that follow instructions perfectly. They're the ones that think independently, move decisively, and aren't afraid to try something that's never been done before.

Every chapter in this book came from watching owners do exactly that. They didn't wait for permission. They didn't need a case study to prove it would work. They saw a problem, proposed a solution, and executed with conviction.

That's innovation. Not the technology. Not the automation. Not the fancy processes. The willingness to do something different.

•••

Knowledge and Action

We started this book with a quote from Bernard of Clairvaux: "There are those who seek knowledge in order to serve; that is Love."

We wrote this book to serve you. To give you frameworks, stories, and tools that make building an eight-figure pharmacy more achievable.

But knowledge alone won't get you there. Action will.

The pharmacies we featured in this book, Riverside, BigRx, Art of Care, Hudson, Beacon, RX Compounding, all of them, they didn't just read about these principles. They implemented them. They made mistakes. They adjusted. They kept moving.

Your pharmacy has the potential to be in the next edition of this book. Not because you copied someone else's path, but because you forged your own.

•••

Final Challenge

So here's my final challenge to you: Pick one idea from

this book. Just one. The one that resonated most. The one that made you think, "That could work for us."

Now give yourself two weeks. Not two months. Not "when things calm down." Two weeks.

Execute it. Test it. Learn from it. Then pick the next one.

That's how you build an eight-figure pharmacy. Not with one giant leap, but with a series of deliberate, focused experiments that compound over time.

We're rooting for you. We're here if you need us. And we can't wait to see what you build.

Now go make it happen.

•••

One Last Thing

Remember that email I asked you to send me at the beginning of this book? If you sent it, I replied. If you didn't, it's not too late.

This isn't just a book. It's the start of a relationship. We're building a community of innovative pharmacy owners who refuse to accept the status quo.

Email: Jonathan@tjmlabs.com

Subject: I finished the book

Body:

> "Hi Jonathan,
>
> I just finished The Innovative Pharmacy and here's what I'm implementing first: [tell me the one thing you're committing to].
>
> [Your name]"

Or text me: 347-861-1051

I read every message. And I reply to every one.

Let's build something extraordinary together.

Made in the USA
Coppell, TX
20 March 2026

73839850R00104